THE RIDE OF MY LIFE

THE RIDE OF MY LIFE

A Fight to Survive Pancreatic Cancer

BOB BROWN

iUniverse, Inc.
Bloomington

The Ride of My Life
A Fight to Survive Pancreatic Cancer

iUniverse books may be ordered through booksellers or by contacting:

iUniverse
1663 Liberty Drive
Bloomington, IN 47403
www.iuniverse.com
1-800-Authors (1-800-288-4677)

Edited by Erica Dhawan
Cover art by Katie Crilley

ISBN: 978-1-4620-6327-7 (sc)
ISBN: 978-1-4620-6329-1 (hc)
ISBN: 978-1-4620-6328-4 (ebk)

Library of Congress Control Number: 2011942255

Printed in the United States of America

iUniverse rev. date: 01/07/2012

For Taylor and Colton

Introduction

My name is Bob Brown. I have pancreatic cancer. Technically, I am a pancreatic cancer survivor, since I'm still alive as I write this. According to the American Cancer Society, 1,596,670 new cases (of which over 40,000 will be pancreatic) are expected to be diagnosed in 2011. That's over 4,300 people every day who receive a diagnosis of cancer, and thus begin a frightening, all-consuming journey into the world of this life-threatening disease.

This is the story of my battle with cancer:

- What it's like to hear the words "inoperable," "pancreatic," and "cancer" describe your illness,
- How I learned to navigate the medical community and its many options,
- How I received the gift of a new perspective on life,
- How I decided to never give up, and most of all . . .
- How to fight to stay alive.

Before

Before I came down with this disease, I was just a regular 50-year-old guy with an absolutely wonderful life—a supportive, loving wife, Linda; two endearing children—Taylor (my affectionate 5-year-old daughter) and Colton (my 3-year-old "discovering life face first" son); a fulfilling job of eight years as the president of a terrific small consumer goods company and all the perks that came from that hard work . . . the house, the travel, the cars (including the obligatory 50-year-old guy car: a 2001 dark red Corvette); a small group of longtime friends; dinners at wonderful restaurants, Broadway shows, lots of ball games. You get the picture. I was very happy, laughed easily, was quick with a joke, and had a kind word to say about everyone.

I graduated from Bucknell University, became a CPA, and after working the obligatory stint in public accounting (highlighted by obtaining my CPA license in NJ and PA), I transitioned into private corporate life as CFO of the US division of a well-known Italian olive oil company. It was there that I was fortunate enough to branch out beyond the financial management ropes, gain a broader knowledge of business, and learn the philosophies, strategies, and tactics for running a successful consumer goods company.

I took those lessons and moved on to a smaller Italian foods company as vice president. After one year, I was promoted to president, and served there for three additional years. I thoroughly enjoyed working for Italian-owned companies. The trips were some of the most enriching you could imagine, and I was fortunate enough to have visited Italy over 40 times in my career. The Italian people are some of the warmest, friendliest, and most full-of-life people I have ever met. They have a delightfully colorful outlook on life that seeks to balance work, family, and pleasure.

I left the world of Italian foods for a different kind of consumer product when I accepted the position of president of the US division of a British-owned fine art materials manufacturer. While many of the skills needed were similar, the difference between working for the Italians and the British was enormous. The Italians were intensely passionate, yelling much of the time. The Brits were far more reserved. I always knew where I stood with the Italians since they were either warmly hugging and kissing me on both cheeks, or deliberately avoiding all contact. The gents from the UK were more even keeled, quiet, almost secretive. The differences went on and on. I loved working in the international arena, and I loved working for those companies.

From a personal standpoint, I married young, had a loving marriage turn sour, and suffered through an amazingly amicable divorce. At 35 years old, despite professional success, I felt that I had failed miserably in life. That's when I met Linda. We had both participated in a charity bachelor/bachelorette auction for the benefit of the Big Brothers/Big Sisters organization. We were each auctioned off to the highest bidder (I went for more money than Linda by the way), and the plan called for the winning bidders and their bachelor or bachelorettes to go out on one giant group date later that month to Pegasus, a fancy restaurant located at the Meadowlands Racetrack. The problem was that by the time the date night arrived, Linda and I had begun dating each other. So there we were, entertaining other people in front of each other. That story alone could fill a short book, and it's always a big hit when someone asks us how we met each other, but suffice it to say that Linda felt I was entertaining my date a bit too enthusiastically. Linda and I dated for several years while she patiently waited for my sorrow and indecision to lift. We were married in 1998, welcomed our daughter in 2002, and our son in 2004.

By January 2008, I had just finished a difficult three years, first caring (with my brothers) for my 80-year-old mother, who was gradually deteriorating with chronic obstructive pulmonary disease (COPD), then settling her affairs after her death at 83 in March 2007. She lived a long, satisfying life and was blessed with children and grandchildren who loved her, especially my little girl Taylor, the only granddaughter . . . the daughter she never had . . . *the one I was supposed to be!*

My father passed away in 1988, at 64, from lymphoma . . . too young. After he died, I made sure to live my life to the fullest, not too crazy, still providing for the future, but never putting off what I could do in the present. My folks never went to college, though they made sure that their three boys did. They lived for their family, the way their generation always did. They had lifelong friends—60 and 70 year friendships! They laughed a lot and gave their sons a lot more than they ever had. In death, their generous estate passed to us, still providing. Wow.

I miss them every day.

Our Last Great Stress-free Day

"I want to thank everyone for coming tonight. It's a testament to Linda that so many of you have come. Some from far away, some from right around the corner. But I know that you all share in the joy of celebrating her fortieth birthday. Baby, I love you with all my heart, and I wish you the happiest of birthdays."

Over the years, Linda has given me some of the most extravagant, generous, and fun presents you could imagine. I'm talking the kinds that draw oohs and aahs and are envied by all of the guys I know. Hell, some of them wish they were married to her based on that alone (not to mention a host of other very attractive features). She's given me a Nascar driving experience at Pocono Motor Speedway, tickets to the final all-star game at the old Yankee Stadium, and the ultimate: For our annual four day trip to the Saratoga Jazz Festival, she rented a $200,000 James Bond Aston Martin for me to drive. Like I said, really cool presents!

Of course, I couldn't touch that. But I had planned this party for months, and while the party itself wasn't a surprise (an addition that would have increased the difficulty factor exponentially—and out of my range), it did provide for some surprise guests and events. One of those was getting her parents, sister and brother, and their families to fly in from the west, and one was my birthday gift itself, which was a trip to Flemington, NJ, widely recognized in these parts as the fur capital of the world. That's where she picked out her first fur, a full-length mink coat that looks gorgeous on her. Now if we could get her into the Aston Martin with the mink . . .

"So if you'd all join with me . . . happy birthday to you, happy birthday to you, happy birthday dear Linda, happy birthday to you . . ."

Must Have Been Something I Ate

A few days after the party, I get a severe bout of diarrhea. Imagine that, spending all that money on catering, and they poison the host! The diarrhea goes on for a few days, then a week. A visit to a medi-center ends with prescriptions for Cipro and Flagell (the gold standard for all gastrointestinal issues). When the symptoms continue into the second week, I go to my regular doctor, who's an hour away, and he confirms the treatment program.

During the second week, I develop this ridiculous bout of itching—my hands, my feet, my scalp, my . . . well, everything. I look like a strung out dog with fleas. I stay awake in bed, scratching constantly with zero relief, running to the bathroom every 30 minutes. I keep trying to work, but it becomes increasingly difficult. The itching won't subside, which is initially pretty funny to my staff, but in truth, I cannot concentrate.

There is something strange about how I'm feeling. This itching isn't on the surface of my skin, it's coming from . . . *inside me*. The diarrhea is well beyond a real pain in the . . . well, you fill in the joke. Why aren't I getting any better? What the hell is wrong with me?

It's now February 3, 2008, and I watch the Giants win the Super Bowl by myself (Linda was also sick, with the flu, in bed), wrapped in blankets, on my couch, utterly miserable . . . until THE CATCH, and the win. It's my first real joy in the last few weeks.

The next day, I turn yellow. Not chicken, or coward. My whole body turns yellow, like a mud-covered lemon. I'm thinking this can't be good.

But I'm wrong. In fact, it's the first miracle. It gets me to the hospital.

Boy, I Hate Hospitals, Except When You're Sick

Since Linda is still in bed with the flu, I drive to our local hospital alone, telling her that I'll call her when I know something. The ER nurse asks me what I am there for.

"Hello, in case you haven't noticed, I'm like . . . YELLOW! And I have an industrial strength case of diarrhea."

"How long have you been yellow?"

"Since this morning."

"How long have you had diarrhea?"

"Two weeks."

"Been out of the country recently?"

"Yes, to the UK."

"How about India, Far East?"

"I had Indian and Chinese food in the UK, does that count?"

After that, considering how I'm feeling, it all starts to sound like the teacher in the PEANUTS© comics, "Whah, whah whah, whah whah whah." They admit me to the hospital that day.

The GI doctor assigned to me is Dr. Serious, a fairly young, confident doctor who takes me through the potential causes of my distress. His approach seems thorough, but lacks any real compassion or humor. He orders a series of tests, and after eliminating more benign illnesses like hepatitis, they find that I have a stricture of the main bile duct—in essence, a narrowing of that critical tube that carries bile to the intestines. That translates into a backing up of bile, which causes my itching, diarrhea, and fruity-colored skin. With a relatively simple procedure, we can insert a stent and relieve the symptoms.

"No food after midnight tonight, your ERCP (an endoscopic procedure) is scheduled for noon," says Dr. S, without even a small smile.

The next day, there's an emergency and my ERCP keeps getting pushed back further and further, eventually being rescheduled for the following day.

"Nothing other than clear liquids until the procedure," the doctor tells me again.

"I'm getting more than a little hungry here," I say to whoever would listen to me. No one does.

"Enjoy your broth!" the food service orderly cheerfully declares.

It tastes just like this whole situation; it sucks. It does match my skin color though.

The next day, my procedure goes perfectly, and soon all of my symptoms disappear.

"Okay, this wasn't so bad." Famous last words.

Excuse Me, Did You Just Say . . .

"Tumors?"

Dr. Serious tells Linda and me that while they successfully treated my current crisis, bile duct strictures don't just occur naturally in the body. They are almost always caused by tumors pushing against the duct and restricting the flow. Kind of like stepping on a garden hose. And the tumors are usually in the pancreas. Oh no please, not the pancreas! Talk about getting hosed. I know that pancreatic cancer is very, very bad. Quick, unpleasant deaths. When I was in my teens, a cousin of mine got the diagnosis. Three weeks later, he was dead. He was 44.

They hadn't seen any tumors on the CT scans, my CA19-9 blood markers for pancreatic cancer were normal, and the scrapings from the inside of my bile duct were negative. All good news.

"Mr. Brown, we need to keep looking. I want to do an endoscopic ultrasound directly on your pancreas tomorrow. We need to find out for certain. Nothing to eat after midnight, clear liquids only until then."

My food service guy is already smiling again. I'm not.

Linda climbs into the bed with me. "We're going to get through this," she says as we hug each other.

I stir slightly on the gurney in the recovery room; the nurse notices and comes to my side. She leans down and says, "Mr. Brown, no tumors." I am still groggy, but I sigh and say "Thank you." It was said to my nurse, but it was meant for everyone . . . in the world!

I start to cry, and don't stop for a while.

Linda and I are relieved by the continued good news. No tumors in my pancreas! That's a big bullet to dodge. I get discharged from the hospital, thank the doctors for getting me through the crisis, and tell them that with due respect, I will follow up with my regular GI doctor from this point forward.

So, what the heck is wrong with me? What caused the stricture? How did I come in here with a bad case of the runs and leave here looking for cancerous tumors?

I take a few days off to recover physically and mentally and make an appointment with our family GI doctor.

Good to See You Again

Dr. Goodguy has been our family GI doctor for 10 years. He's a fit, young guy (isn't everybody younger now?) with a full head of curly brown hair that tracks down past his ears. All the nurses love him. He's smart as a tack, thorough, and personable, and calls his patients directly, introducing himself by his first name only. Like your close friend calling.

We were referred to him by our family GP when Linda was finding blood in her stool daily. That was 10 years ago, 6 months after we were married.

After a colonoscopy revealed some suspicious polyps (which he removed), we anxiously awaited the results. Some days later, we got the call, "Come in to see me as soon as you can." We soon learned that that's doctor code for "I don't want to tell you the results over the telephone," and that's never a good thing.

One of the polyps contained cancerous cells, and while the polyp was out, there was no way to be certain that cancer cells hadn't invaded the colon at the site of the polyp's stem. The doctor's recommendation was to strongly consider surgery to remove 12 inches of her colon, 6 inches on each side of the spot. Colon cancer, white, Caucasian, female, 31. The statistics for her to get colon cancer didn't even seem to exist, yet here we were, she had it. And she had to decide to either have elective major surgery, or do nothing and hope that the cancer never came back.

After some heartfelt deliberations, Linda decided to have the surgery—full, open surgery on her belly and abdomen, which would leave her with a "boobs to pubes" scar. Not easy for a young woman. Her surgeon turned out to be a woman who completely understood this and used plastic surgery techniques to close her incision. Her scar is pencil point thin and barely visible. The surgery went well and she was a real trooper during the recovery. She has been closely monitored ever since, and today she is a long-term colon cancer survivor.

When we walk into the office, Dr. G has already reviewed my records and seems just as perplexed as we are. Seems like all good news, but we need to keep looking. He says that I need to prepare for surgery to at least remove the small section of the bile duct that has narrowed and is being kept open by the stent. He orders two MRIs: a normal one for the abdominal cavity, and a special one for the pancreas. He also gives me the name of the chief of GI surgical oncology at Hackensack Medical Center and tells me to make an appointment.

"Nice to see you again, Doc, too bad it wasn't for something more pleasant, like a colonoscopy," I say as we leave his office.

The MRIs are pretty tough—claustrophobic, loud, uncomfortable, and over 45 minutes long. Two seconds after I'm in the tube, my face starts to itch in several places. Of course, I can't scratch because my arms are down at my sides and there's not enough room to bring my hands up. This is going to be fun. At one point, the technician asks me to slow down my breathing to a specific rhythm. Finally succeeding after several minutes of trying to get it exactly right, the tech says, "Great, now keep that pace up for seven minutes while we take some more pictures."

What does he think I am, a ventilator?

Roller Coaster—Get on Board

Webster's dictionary defines roller coaster as "an elevated railway with cars and sudden sharp turns and drops" (noun), and also "anything resembling a roller coaster with behavior, events or experiences characterized by sudden and extreme changes, such as an emotional roller coaster" (noun).

If you're from the northeast, particularly the New York metropolitan area, you know that the Cyclone at Coney Island is one of the all-time greatest roller coasters in the world. Despite the fact that it was built more than 80 years ago, and has been surpassed in size many times over by the giant steel and wooden super coasters of today, it remains one of the "must rides" for coaster enthusiasts the world over. You walk up to it, and you can't believe how small it is. This can't possibly be what everyone talks about. There must be another Cyclone down the street somewhere. After going on all of the newer coasters, this looks like it belongs in the kiddie park. Then you get on, take that first drop, and you know. A couple of minutes later, it's simply, "My gosh, that was incredible . . . wanna go again?" That's the Cyclone.

My first ride was when I was probably 9 or 10 years old. My mom took me to Coney Island for the day, just the two of us. My brothers were much older and weren't all that interested in going to amusement parks with their mom and kid brother. The first thing I did was play the game where you get to throw baseballs at plates, trying to break as many as you could. Heck, I'd been breaking plates at home for a long time, and I never won any prizes for it! Then it was on to the big stuff, the Bobsled, the Wonder Wheel, and finally, the Cyclone. Most of Coney Island's amusements are long gone now. But the Cyclone lives on.

As I walk into the examination room for my first set of MRIs, I don't realize it at the time, but I'm about to get on the Cyclone again, last row.

And I'm not getting off anytime soon.

The First Big Drop

Dr. Supersmart, the surgeon, has an office full of people, and the waiting room walls are lined with reprints of magazine articles and covers extolling his skills and high standing. He seems to have a pretty good reputation. I read through his brochure about the various ailments that he treats and his methods of surgeries, paying particular attention to the sections on diseases of the pancreas. I feel that we're in the right place. This feels good. After a rather short wait, we're called in and he comes into the examination room. He's African American with a pleasant demeanor and a vocabulary that immediately sends us searching for the dictionaries. Linda and I are fairly intelligent people and we can't follow anything he's saying. It's way over our heads. After a few minutes with him, my head hurts.

"Doctor, I'm having trouble following you," I reply, clearly lying since I'm not following him at all.

"Could you maybe explain it in simpler terms?"

"There appears to be a slight shadow in your pancreas on the MRI," he says very matter of factly.

"What does it mean?" Linda and I ask simultaneously.

"Well, it could be leftover pancreatitis from your recent illness, or it could be something more. Let's wait a couple of weeks and redo the same tests to see if the shadow shrinks or disappears."

As those weeks go by, I'm confident that this is nothing serious. I feel much better; the doctors at the hospital have already scoped my pancreas and declared it tumor free. I'm really not worried at all.

Three weeks later, we repeat the tests and he confirms that there definitely is a mass in the neck of my pancreas. My journey has just taken a bad turn. He immediately schedules me for major surgery, but first I need to have a biopsy to determine exactly what type of tumor we're dealing with.

Linda and I are still relatively calm at this point. The tumor is very small and all of the other tests and markers have shown it to be negative. We've caught this early, there's been no spread, and we're confident that even if this is cancerous, it can be successfully dealt with. But I've just been hit with the first punch.

The biopsy doctor, Dr. Optimism, is a great guy who reviews my records, tells me that I look great, and assures me that we'll get to the bottom of the mystery with this test. He gives me a world of confidence before the biopsy. That is, until I wake up from the anesthesia.

"Mr. Brown, the tumor visually appears to be malignant. I've seen many of these, and it certainly appears to be that way. The biopsy results will tell us for certain. I'll contact you as soon as I know."

Two days later, Dr. O calls me at home in the evening. Here we go. I put the call on speaker so Linda can listen in, take a deep breath, and wait for his next words.

"Mr. Brown, this is not a telephone call that I make easily. We took a lot of tissue samples from your tumor, enough for 20 slides. In addition to the pathologist, I reviewed the slides myself. They are all negative for cancer."

I start crying again. "Doctor, that is great news!" I say through the tears. "What do we do now?"

"We have to do the biopsy again to be sure. I've scheduled you for the day after tomorrow."

We speak with Linda's sister, Laura, who is a pulmonologist and head of in-patients at the VA hospital in Cheyenne, Wyoming. She is our in-house expert and has always been there to put medical mumbo-jumbo into English.

She says that the negative biopsy is not uncommon, and that we should be prepared if the results of the second one are different from the first.

The following day is a good day. Despite the fact that everyone tells me to be cautious, I am moderately optimistic that the additional biopsy will confirm the first one. A small group of my close friends schedule a night out to send me off to my surgery with the good wishes of the group. As I walk into the bar, I have more bounce in my step, my head is high, and I have a smile on my face. One by one, my friends are pleasantly stunned to hear the good news, and although the road ahead is still murky, the tenor of the night changes to one of optimistic celebration, with good food and toasts all around.

My support group is growing. And believe me, a large and committed support group is something that becomes critical to your well-being.

That Was a Good Run

I almost forgot to tell you—my boss from the UK is in town for our regular bi-monthly business meetings. We review the state of business (like most other industries, not so good), the status of new products and other projects, and a host of other peripheral issues related to the US division.

The new boss is a tough executive who's been cutting costs in the worldwide group over the past two years in order to make the company achieve its profit goals. We don't see eye to eye on many issues.

As I said, I have been the president of the US division of a UK art materials company for the past eight years and have successfully built an efficient, lean, close-knit team that is now managing about double the sales as when I first arrived.

It's a great job that has allowed me to work with customers large and small, travel throughout the US and the globe, and oversee all aspects of a thriving consumer goods business. I often compare it to being the manager of the New York Yankees. When the company is doing well, I receive a lot of credit, and when the going gets tough, I take much of the heat. And like the manager of the Yanks, I expect that one day there will be a change, and I'll be out as president.

I just didn't expect it to be a week before going through the most important medical test of my life. My boss informs me that my job is being made redundant. That's Euro speak for "You're out." He will run the overall operation from the UK and save my costs (which were the highest in the company).

While I haven't yet gotten an official diagnosis of what is ailing me, I have been in and out of work over the past six weeks, and it is clear to everyone that the doctors are searching for cancer.

So it seems like a pretty rotten time to terminate someone, but you know what? It turns out to be a true blessing in disguise. It removes the day-to-day stress of work, and it gives me the time and energy to fight for my life.

I wouldn't quite classify this as a miracle, but it turns out to be another event that seems cruel and unfair at the time, but ends up being a piece of good fortune.

You Think You Had a Bad Week?

By now, you should be realizing that I'm able to find something positive and (frequently) funny in most everything that comes my way.

As I sit on the all-too-familiar gurney waiting for Dr. Optimism to give me my second pre-biopsy pep talk, I start to fully comprehend the scope of this test. Confirm the negative results and we're still removing a pancreatic mass, but one that is benign. If the test comes back positive, then I have pancreatic cancer. No more looking for something, we will have found it. I'm not making any more witty quips. I'm damned nervous and scared.

The doctor explains that we need to know for sure, and that he's going to take as much tissue as necessary, working with a pathologist in the procedure room who will analyze the tissue as we go. I tell him that I appreciate that, and that I'm ready . . . let's go.

When I wake up, Linda is sitting next to me. I ask where the doctor is and she says that he's doing another procedure, and that he'll be a while. "Great, now we've got to wait," I sigh, and I look into her eyes. She's spoken to the doctor already. She knows, then I know.

"It's positive. You have cancer," she says with a look on her face that I had never seen before. Then she says, "No matter what, we will get through this," with a conviction that carries me to this day.

I lose my breath and my ability to focus for a while. I'm starting to cry again, and I can assure you that for once, I don't find anything positive or remotely funny. I immediately think of Linda and the kids. How will we all cope? Can I actually beat this type of cancer? Does anybody? How long will I have? How will they move on, what will their life be like without me? Will Taylor and Colton even remember me? My mind keeps reverting to just one thought: I'm a dead man walking.

Dr. O appears and fills us in on what they found, echoing what Linda told me a short while ago. He continues to somehow talk optimistically, but he adds something that he hadn't told my wife. The surgery is off. I now have to see the chief of oncology instead. It seems that my small, early-detected tumor is wrapped around the superior mesenteric artery. There is no surgery to remove a tumor with that complication. So you see, I don't just have pancreatic cancer. I have *Stage III Inoperable Pancreatic Cancer*. Bottom of the coaster.

Linda drives us home from the hospital. We don't say much to one another, except some absurdly trivial stuff like what we should make the kids for dinner. Or maybe whether we should have Amanda, our nanny, take them to her house for the night, rather than having them see their dad as a complete basket case. About halfway home, we silently reach out and clasp hands. We don't let go for a long time.

I was terminated from my job and received the worst possible medical diagnosis in the span of a few days. Last week, I was Bob Brown, living and enjoying my life as I knew it, preparing for a fight if there was one coming. Now, after two short, serious conversations, I am being propelled to a completely different world. One where I will be in for a real fight—for my identity and for my life.

How was your week?

Statistics Don't Lie, Do They?

As most everyone knows, the Internet is a wealth of information at your fingertips. Whether those fingers are flying at 90+ wpm, or more like my 4-5 finger hunt-and-peck approach, you can find just about anything you need in the glorious world of cyberspace.

What I find out that first day post-diagnosis is this: Although there are 300+ million people in the US, "only" about 40,000 people a year are diagnosed with pancreatic cancer, so it remains one of the more rare cancers, yet one of the most deadly.

You cannot get a cancer with a worse survival rate than pancreatic. Survival rates are often quoted in five-year rates. If you survive beyond five years, then often you're considered cured. The war on cancer has provided some stunning progress. Here are some of the recent five-year rates of survival:

Prostate: 98.8%
Breast: 86.4%
Hodgkin's: 85.1%
Kidney: 61.8%
Colon: 61.7%
Ovarian: 55%

And some of the poorer ones:

Brain: 32%
Stomach: 23.8%
Lung: 15%

And mine:

Pancreatic: 5%

I also learn that the only patients who have a chance to survive pancreatic cancer are those that are able to have their tumors surgically removed. Then the survival rates increase into the 30 percent range. But mine . . . inoperable. I know I've said this before, but this definitely is not good news. I think I'll take a break from Internet research for a while.

I turn off the laptop and go outside to our backyard deck. It's cold and I stare out at the brown, end-of-winter lawn and start to dream about how beautiful it will look in the spring, green and lush, filled with new life. I wonder if I'll ever see that again.

Later that night, our family repeats a nightly ritual, getting the kids into their jammies, and all piling into Mom and Dad's bed, "The Big Bed." There, we talk, snuggle, and play under the covers before delivering some calm-down time and shuttling them off to their own beds for the night. It's something that all of us look forward to, and our customary group hug means more to me that night than any of the others before.

It gives me comfort, it gives me perspective, it gives me purpose, and it gives me strength.

Let the Battle Begin

I have never uttered the words "Why me?" I think I might be entitled to, given the stats, given all the good that was going on in my life, given that I was more than just a basically good person, given just about everything. But you know what? It's meaningless, and more importantly, it's a useless waste of energy.

Who cares why, when, where, how or what if? They don't matter. What does matter, and what doesn't change, is that I do have cancer. Period. Exclamation point!

Now I have to beat it. Despite the odds.

If you've ever seen the crazy Jim Carrey movie *Dumb and Dumber*, there's a scene where his total-loser character asks the girl he's smitten with:

"What do think the chances are that you and I will end up together?"
"Not good."
"You mean not good, like one in a hundred?"
"I'd say more like one in a million."
"So, you're saying that I've got a chance!"

That's how I look at this. A slim chance is still a chance. One that I have to maximize. You hear a lot of interesting comments about statistics when you get cancer. The ones I like best are:

"Statistics are the results of what's happened to other people, not you."

"Every person's case is different, at different stages. Statistics are for the entire universe of cases. No one statistic can apply to your individual case."

"When the chance of rain is 80%, that may be statistically true, but it only rains on you if you're under the clouds . . . stay in the sun!"

I live by this one: "Even though only one in twenty who has this disease survives, I'm going to be that one." Period. Exclamation point!

I decide that I finally have to let my many friends and colleagues know what is transpiring. Many of them knew different pieces of the story so far, and now that we definitively know that it's cancer, it's time to let everyone know the details.

The subject line of the email is "Let the Battle Begin." I really should have replaced the word "battle" with "war," for fighting cancer involves many separate battles. Some you win and others you lose, but you cannot lose sight of the war. My email explains that over the course of several weeks and numerous tests, I have indeed been diagnosed with inoperable pancreatic cancer. I am to begin chemotherapy immediately with the goal of shrinking the tumor enough to become operable. I remain optimistic and confident that I will beat this disease. Physically, I am feeling great, and I thank everyone for their love, prayers, and support.

Most everyone responds back to me fairly quickly. There are emails and cards, letters and fruit baskets, all with the same message: "We love your attitude (particularly the part about let the battle begin), let us know whatever you need, and it'll be done."

Thus begins the start of an ongoing communication forum between me and an ever-expanding circle of my family, friends, friends of friends, and sometimes even total strangers.

So This is Chemotherapy

We choose Hackensack University Medical Center in Hackensack, NJ, as the location for my treatment program. HUMC is a nationally recognized, top-flight medical center where my wife and my mom received expert quality care throughout their various medical journeys.

Linda and I arrive for my initial chemo session on a bright sunny morning, a few days after meeting the director of GI oncology and listening to him lay out the plan of attack. Our first stop is the waiting room. What strikes me is how *crowded* it is. The place has seating for at least 50-60 people, and all of the seats are taken. Many of the people look terribly worn down, their skin grayish in color, their hair thinning or completely gone. The looks on their faces are a blend of worry and weariness, sprinkled with a touch of dread. Their ages run the spectrum from young adult to the elderly, and across all ethnicities. So many of them are women. Cancer truly is an equal opportunity disease. Thank God there are no children here. The conversations are hushed, except for the volunteers who cheerfully bring coffee and treats, trying to bring a level of normalcy to a very surreal place.

I get called into a small room, and after having my vitals taken and blood drawn by a technician, I'm directed into a smaller waiting room, then finally into one of the exam rooms to wait for my doctor. It's a fine-tuned process, and while it works pretty well to funnel us through to the doctors, it's quite impersonal. After a short wait, Dr. Direct enters the room. He's in his forties, experienced, smart, and personable. He asks about our children, what we like to do, and even offers a little insight into his own family and advice about our upcoming trip to Disney World at summer's end. What I don't sense from him is any level of confidence about my situation.

"Okay, your blood counts look good, today we begin," he declares.

Linda and I make a few side jokes and I tell him that I am ready to go. We are very upbeat and enthusiastic.

He says that he usually doesn't have patients arriving for their first chemo session in such good spirits. He's surprised, but feels that a good attitude is important for making it through the chemotherapy program.

"Listen, Doctor, so far I haven't done anything to fight this disease. Today is a good day; today I start to fight back."

He smiles and tells me to be easy on the nurses. Then he points to a door at the end of the hallway with no sign on it.

"Go on through to the Infusion Center, good luck," he says with a slight smile.

Attitude Matters

The first things you notice when you pass through that door are the chairs. Recliners actually, all lined up neatly around the perimeter of the infusion room. It seems that the medical community wants very much to make you feel at home while they're pumping you full of toxic poisons.

There are about 30 stations, each with a recliner for the patient and a much less comfortable guest chair for the caregiver. It's as if the loved ones don't need that same level of comfort. There's a small six-inch TV attached to an arm that swings from the wall, and a hospital-room-type table that can move up and down and hold your stuff. On each side are curtains that can be pulled to give you a degree of privacy. Oh, and there's also a giant IV pole with many, many hooks, next to each chair.

I'm directed to chair number eight, Linda's favorite number, a good sign. Chair number seven would have been better. It was a corner spot with more privacy, with room for Linda and I to spread out. But another patient, a young woman who was having a violent reaction to one of the medications, was already occupying that chair. Her face is swollen to double its original size and the nurses are working frantically to counteract it with Benadryl. Not exactly the type of confidence-inducing activity that you want going on right next door.

My nurse comes over and begins to illustrate the chemo process. She's young (isn't everybody when you're 50?), pretty, intelligent, and speaks in a very soothing style. She extolls the virtues of my doctor, mentions how lucky I am that my cancer has been detected early, and lays out the details of how this chemo thing works. Then she communicates how important it is for a patient to have a good attitude when going through chemo, that those with the best attitudes often have the best outcomes, and she feels mine is terrific. When I challenge her about attitudes really having an impact on the patient, she says that she sees hundreds of patients a week, and "believe me when I tell you that attitude matters."

My chemo sessions will be once a week for six weeks. Each session will be about eight hours long, and I'll be receiving two different chemo drugs (Cisplatin and Gemcytabine), along with a bevy of other meds to protect me from the side effects of the chemo. There are meds to prevent nausea, others to prevent rashes, and my body needs to be flushed clean for a couple of hours before and after the chemo to ensure that my kidneys won't shut down from the treatments.

The nurse gets my meds, shows them to me, and starts arranging them on my pole. Several of the bags have that bright red warning sticker on them. You know, the one with the skull and crossbones, highlighting the severity of what's inside. I guess I should have one of those labels permanently attached to my belly, since what's going on in there is pretty severe. In no time at all, she inserts an IV into the back of my wrist and away we go. The first couple of hours on the drip are fairly easy, and we pass the time by reading and watching TV. After about three hours, I'm ready to receive the first chemo drug, and I will tell you that it's a bizarre and difficult experience. As with much of the cancer battle, there's a mental aspect that must be dealt with. You sit and watch as this poison enters your blood stream. You begin to imagine the medicine attacking the cancer cells, while at the same time trying to concentrate on the physical feelings. On one hand, you hope to feel nothing, while on the other hand, you hope to feel something that would indicate it's working. Of course, that's not going to happen; in fact, it will be the other way around. Whatever is working will be imperceptible to you, while whatever you do actually feel will be side effects, and they will almost always definitely be bad.

The room is filled with activity and the oncology nurses have their hands full, as patients are constantly coming and going. It seems as though everyone else's treatments are a lot shorter than mine. As the hours drag on and the chemo builds in my system, I definitely feel worse. Linda can tell when the chemo enters my system, as my skin color changes immediately. Luckily, I don't get nauseous, but I am constantly running to the bathroom to expel the large quantities of fluids that I'm taking in.

About halfway through the day, another volunteer comes pushing a snack cart containing sandwiches, fruit, juices, soup, etc. I grab a ham sandwich and a couple of sugar cookies. As I wolf them down I notice that not many of my fellow chemo buddies are eating much at all. Maybe they're on to something here. After a few bites, I realize that they are wise not to be eating the snacks.

Then it's over, eight-and-a-half hours after it started. Including the pre-chemo evaluation, we've been here for the better part of 10 hours. The nurse disconnects me and issues a set of discharge instructions, telling me what to do if and when various side effects happen.

"You did great today. I know it was a long day, but hang in there. We'll try to make it move a little more quickly next week. See you then."

"Thanks," I reply. "Don't worry about how long it takes, I'll be here."

This is where the fight is.

Hey, This Isn't So Bad, or Is It?

As the weeks tick by, the routine becomes pretty standard: get to the hospital, check in, have my vitals checked, see my oncologist, who reviews the results to make sure that my blood counts are good enough to survive another treatment, then on to the infusion room for the goods. Linda and I bring her laptop with comedy DVDs and matching pairs of headphones. We sit there for much of the day laughing out loud at the movies while the chemo courses through my bloodstream, blasting away at the bad, causing collateral damage to the good, and making me feel pretty darn lousy.

Although I am not experiencing any of the more harsh side effects (like nausea, vomiting, diarrhea, hair loss, mouth sores, etc.), I am beginning to feel run down. The cumulative effect of the weekly visits is causing an overall tiredness that seems to be coming from my insides. I'm still eating well and not losing weight. Overall, I seem to be physically tolerating the treatments quite well. Anyone who sees me finds it hard to believe that I'm undergoing treatment for PC, since I appear so healthy. This is going about as well as I could hope for.

But the very sad reality of the situation has begun to sink in. This is not some macho battle like I've been thinking of it and portraying it to my friends and family. Whenever I was sick before, I'd go to the doctor (or on rare occasions, the hospital), get some medicine, and be on my way to getting better. Whatever it was, I'd go to the doctor, and I'd start to get well. But this is not like any ailment that I've ever had before. This is cancer. Not just any doctor can treat it. Not just any medicine works. Not everyone gets better.

The reality of the war is becoming clearer now. While the drugs are fighting their invisible war on my tumor, the real battles are being fought from the neck up. It's become a test of faith, confidence, physical and mental toughness, or as my dad was always fond of saying, "intestinal fortitude." Guts, plain and simple. But I've never faced anything like this before. I've never had my survival qualities or abilities tested like this. I've never had to look deep inside my core to see what I'm made of. I have no idea if I can get through this, and I certainly don't know if I'll make it out of this alive. Throughout all of this, Linda is with me every step of the way. We don't talk much about the prognosis. We focus on the very short-term issues, like the treatment days, how many down, how many to go. Am I taking the anti-side-effect meds? How are the kids doing with all of this? Can we get Amanda, our nanny, to stay late this coming treatment day?

Of course Amanda can stay late. She's been with us for a long while now and she's become part of our family. What was always a fairly standard 8-to-6 day for her has become more hectic and unpredictable. She doesn't flinch, and continues to be a consistent, wonderful, stabilizing force for Taylor and Colton, keeping them occupied, happy, and well cared for while their parents are in a haze.

Taylor and Colton realize that something is going on with Daddy. They've been watching me as this has transpired.

When my stent became clogged and pain shot through my abdomen until I was unable to catch my breath, they snuggled up to me and rubbed my belly.

When I came home after a grueling day at chemo, they ran up, yelled "Yay, daddy's home!" and gave me a life-affirming hug that lasted until I let go. And most of all, they continued to act like little kids, oblivious to the possibility that those hugs might not be around forever.

When I was first diagnosed, all I could think about was how having young children was such a curse—how they would have such limited memories of me, and how unfair it all was. And they would have the burden of growing up without their real father. Boys, in particular, need a father in their life—someone to show them right from wrong and how to treat a woman—in essence, how to be a good man. I wouldn't be there to do that. I started to have conversations with several of my close friends, asking them to help keep a lookout on my kids, particularly Colton, if things didn't progress as we all hoped.

I would only know the joy of parenthood for a fraction of time, never getting to see them grow up. Never seeing them become teenagers, young adults, mature adults (okay, maybe I wouldn't miss them as teenagers). Never finding out what they would become. Never seeing them marry. Never seeing them have their own children.

But once again, I'm being proven wrong. Having cancer and young children isn't a curse. It's a blessing. You see, whereas older kids might be more independent, my young children need me. They need me to get up in the morning and help them get ready for school, to keep the food coming, and to help with their homework. And little kids are really funny; they keep me laughing my butt off day after day.

Laughter is terrific medicine. Thank God for my kids. They're the fuel for my motivation engine.

So This Was the Reason

Linda and I had been married for less than a year when she was diagnosed with colon cancer. She quickly reached her decision to have her colon resected and was certain that it was the right call.

The surgery was difficult but successful, and her recovery went very well. Her threshold for pain is high, and after eight weeks, she was back at work. Luckily, her doctors did not recommend any type of follow-up chemotherapy. Since her cancer was detected so early, she would be closely monitored with CT scans and colonoscopies.

Physically, she was doing great, but mentally she was facing all of the doubts and questions that cancer patients ask, starting with, "Will it come back?" She struggled mightily with going back to corporate life, instead believing that her true calling might now be more philanthropic in nature, volunteering and helping others. That was something that I couldn't understand until I received the same cancer diagnosis.

As the years have gone by and her tests have gone from quarterly, to semi-annually, to yearly, to now bi-annually, and all the while come back negative, it's become easier for her to accept and embrace that she is indeed a cancer survivor. But the nagging question of why she got cancer took a decade to answer.

"I finally understand why I got cancer," she said to me one day during the early stages of my treatment.

"After all these years of trying to make sense of it, of trying to cope with the stress and the worry of recurrence, of trying to get the answer as to why, it's finally become crystal clear."

"It's so that I would be able to help *you!*"

And the help she gives is everywhere, from accompanying me in every step of the battle, to offering unwavering optimism, to kicking my butt when I become discouraged, and finally taking over the entire process when I hit rock bottom and can't think straight.

No matter how strong you are in the fight, it's essential to have a great corner man (or woman) to counsel, guide, and ultimately help push you through the walls that pop up along the way. I'm very lucky. I have the best.

Family and Friends

My brothers are both older than me. Duane is eight years older and lives with his wife and two sons on Cape Cod in Massachusetts. Gary is six years older, single, and lives in the Catskills in New York.

Since I was born so much later than them, I never really had much of a relationship with them until after I graduated college. Before then, the age difference always kept our interests way apart. When they were approaching their "tween" years, I was a toddler. When I was getting into my own tweens, they were getting ready to leave for college. They never treated me badly, but while they were very close in age, I was always their baby brother. As such, I grew up very much like an only child, being doted on by my mom while my dad worked his tail off in his retail business.

The three boys couldn't be more different. Duane has been successful in the construction industry, first owning a general contracting company and now estimating construction projects. Gary is an accomplished professional musician, having played with many of the jazz greats over the last 40+ years. And me, I've been a CPA who moved on to general executive management in consumer products companies. Like I said, we're all different, yet pretty darn similar when it comes right down to it.

After our dad passed away, my close proximity to my mom, coupled with my business skills, led me to being the son who most helped manage my mom's life in her later years. After she passed, I spent the better part of a year settling her estate and making sure that mom's wishes were carried out in the fastest way. The inheritances went a long way in helping each of our own financial challenges, and my brothers leaned on me heavily when they needed advice on how to best manage their newfound wealth. The baby seemed to be the leader.

When I was diagnosed with cancer, they both came to my support as only family can. It seems as if hardly a day goes by without my hearing from one or both of them. They call, they visit, they listen, and they offer their help in any way that I need. Despite our differences in age and lifestyle, or the geographic distance between us, when the need arises, they are right there. It was very much that way during my mom's final year. That's what family is really all about, isn't it?

Linda's immediate family consists of her parents, sister, brother, and their respective spouses and children. All live in Colorado and Wyoming. They have all offered their love and support to me, and perhaps more importantly, to Linda. She certainly needs it too. Her sister, Laura, is a pulmonologist, and functions as our very own in-house medical expert. While oncology isn't her expertise, she's the one we speak to first after every doctor appointment. She's the one who researches my options. She's able to translate the "medical speak" into layman's terms for us. And while she never sugar coats my situation, many hours on the telephone with her have brought me clarity, comfort, and well-thought-out directions for the journey I'm on. We're incredibly fortunate to have her on our side.

Like most couples, Linda and I have a small group of closest friends. They've reacted very much the same way as my brothers. I'm the first in our group to face a life threatening illness, and I think it's shaken many of them, unfortunately forcing them to look at their own mortalities. Completely overwhelmed at first by my diagnosis, they are always there to talk and help in any way they can.

One brings a home cooked meal to our house every week on chemo day, knowing that we're in no shape to cook for ourselves. Another makes sure to call later in the evenings when he knows that the rest of the family is asleep, and I'm at my most vulnerable. Another makes sure to send humorous emails on a regular basis. Like the song goes, "That's what friends are for."

The one common thread amongst all of the family and friends is the burning question, "How are you doing?"

What can I tell them? That I'm falling apart inside? That I spend most waking hours contemplating my own demise and how my family will cope? How I find it hard to believe that I could be lucky enough to beat this? No, of course not.

"I'm doing okay, hanging in there. So far, so good. Physically it's not as bad as I thought it would be, but mentally it's a strain."

That's an understatement. But I'm just not ready to really let them know how difficult this is becoming.

The End of the First Battle

During the final weeks of my treatments, the side effects start getting more serious. My energy levels are dwindling and I find myself spending more time just resting during the days. I continue to eat fairly well, but my desire for certain foods and drinks has changed. In particular, I don't seem to want to drink as much wine as I did before. And of course, I try to eat more fruits and vegetables, as well as reduce my intake of refined foods.

I receive many suggestions on magical potions and elixirs that friends and acquaintances had heard would help. I just smile and thank them for the ideas, but don't really try any of them. If they were of value, I would have surely known of it.

Just before my treatments end, the stent in my bile duct becomes blocked. It is incredibly painful, causes an infection, and requires a hospital stay, during which the doctors replace it with a fresh one. Apparently, it's not at all uncommon and I should expect that to happen every few months. I haven't been told that before, and it certainly is not something that I look forward to. On the other hand, getting the stent replaced means that I'm still alive. It's just a small price to pay for being able to walk around.

I finish my last treatment amidst very little fanfare. I meet with my oncologist the following week, expecting to get a lot of information and a whole new game plan. Instead, he says that I should get a set of new scans (CT and MRI) and meet with him after they are done. We'll plan the next course of action from there.

Going High Tech

We meet with Dr. Direct several weeks after my chemo has ended and I have had the requisite MRI and CT scans. He declares that we're good to go for the next phase of treatment. The tumor surrounding my artery has not shrunk all that much, but that was to be expected.

"Ouch!"

"But there has been no progression of the disease. You have an appointment tomorrow with Dr. Fire-Away, who is the chief of radiation oncology. He'll explain in much greater detail how the radiation treatments will proceed, but essentially you will receive daily treatment with supplemental chemotherapy once per week. The chemo will make the cancer cells more susceptible to the radiation. Good luck and I'll see you next week for your checkup before the chemo."

Okay, so as I'm starting to realize, it's another mixed bag. On one hand, the cancer has not metastasized, which is extremely good news, and quite uncommon for pancreatic. On the other hand, the chemotherapy hasn't really done anything to the status of my tumor. I expected a better result. I can't believe that the tumor didn't shrink. All tumors shrink when they get chemo'd, don't they?

The enemy is tougher than I first thought. How tough am I?

I wake up the next day in a more energized state. We spoke with Dr. Laura last night and she said that despite the news being below my expectations, moving on to radiation is a positive development. Remember the goal: Get operable before the cancer spreads, remove the tumor, have a chance to live.

I'm still in the fight.

I go to the appointment alone and make my way to the lower level of the hospital where the radiation department is (must be something about keeping the radiation separate from the general population, and well contained. And other than that, it's perfectly safe to fire it into a body). I meet with the next doctor in what's becoming an endless procession. He appears to be in his forties, very professional and doctor-like in his dress, appearance, and overall tone. He has reviewed my file and describes how the radiation treatments will be administered.

"The first week will be primarily devoted to setup. We will take new, more detailed CT scans of your pancreas and create a computer 3D model of it so we can program the radiation treatments to attack the tumor with the greatest degree of accuracy. We will also create an upper body cast for you to lie in when you receive the treatments so we can ensure your exact positioning and stillness during the actual treatments. Finally, you're going to get some small, permanent 'locator' tattoos on your torso. These allow the laser targeting system in the radiation room to determine your correct positioning prior to treatment."

He explains that they will be using intensity modulated radiation therapy (IMRT) and a comprehensive image-guided radiation therapy technique (IGRT). I will receive a total of 28 treatments, each delivering a fraction of the total 5040cGy (actually about 10% more than what's normally prescribed) of radiation that I will be permitted to receive in that area of the body. Apparently, you can't just blast away at the pancreas with unlimited doses of radiation until the tumor dissolves because those levels would destroy just about everything else in their path. And considering where the pancreas is located, we can't just ignore the risks to the stomach, kidneys, and small intestine. Rats!

After listening to all of the technical mumbo jumbo, I ask the doctor how often he's administered this type of neoadjuvant therapy with pancreatic cancer. He immediately knows where I'm heading with my line of questioning. What are the chances that this will work? Will it get me operable?

He's sitting on the edge of the examining table and looking down at me in the guest chair. Until now, he's been the picture of professional confidence, explaining this rocket science to me with the ease of someone who's obviously done it many, many times before. But now he hesitates, seemingly searching for the correct words. Finally, he looks me straight in the eyes.

"Mr. Brown, it is uncommon for us to be in a position to try and turn an inoperable patient into an operable one. Since pancreatic cancer is such an aggressively spreading type, an inoperable tumor almost always metastasizes before it becomes operable. However, despite the time that's passed since your diagnosis, the disease still appears to be confined to your pancreas, and that is allowing us to try through this combination of chemotherapy and radiation."

"How often have you succeeded?"

It seems like a simple question to answer. I expect to hear something like "rarely," "occasionally," or maybe even "frequently" (okay, I don't really expect to hear that). Perhaps he will give me a number, as in "We've succeeded in seven cases."

Instead, he just reiterates the difficult nature of what we are trying to accomplish and the obstacles and risks that are involved. But remember, each patient's results are unique. Not what I am hoping to hear.

It's clear to me that the number is zero.

A Lecture for the Ages

I came across Randy Pausch's *The Last Lecture* very early in its YouTube©
run. So many things happen to you when you have cancer, and one
of them is that you become hypersensitive to any and all peripheral
cancer stories. They're everywhere, from the newspapers, to the
television, to the endless stream of family, friends, and acquaintances
who themselves are getting diagnosed. And now every one of them
hurts your heart.

Dr. Pausch is obviously a stranger to me, but because of this disease we
share, he feels more like a blood brother. I've watched his video a few
times, read the book version, and watched him on several TV specials,
most notably the ones where he is interviewed by Diane Sawyer. Like
most, I am inspired by his courage, devotion to family, and commitment
to making his last days matter for something. But as a fellow pancreatic
cancer patient, I come away with a profound sense of despair and dread.
He was diagnosed in September 2006, and he already had the potential
lifesaving surgery; he'd been lucky in that way. But less than a year
post-surgery, the cancer had come screaming back. Eleven tumors in his
liver, terminal. This brilliant, articulate man who was quickly becoming a
national spokesman for the cause was speaking with the certainty that his
life would soon end. How can this be? Certainly, he has access to the best
physicians and treatments available. Doesn't *anybody* beat this?

I ache for his family—his beautiful, supportive wife, and his young
children who would have so few memories of him. I watch with joy as he
takes them to Walt Disney World®, and wilt with all-too-knowing sadness
as the treatments take more and more life from him. I pray for him. I
follow his daily travails on his blog, watching his CA19-9 cancer marker
number as closely as I had ever watched my favorite ballplayer's stats in
the box scores. When he goes on a hot streak and benefits from a new

41

experimental treatment, my spirits soar. When he suffers setbacks, I'm crushed as well.

I'm the best kind of Randy Pausch fan. I'm walking in the same shoes. I'm pulling for him to get a win.

I need for him to get a win.

I've Got a Job Again

The setup for the radiation treatments is easy, and actually pretty cool. The techs doing the work are very personable and, considering that they're not causing any pain or discomfort, and that we're still in this optimistic period, it all goes well.

First they do the special CT scan, which appears to me like the many I've already had. Then it's the upper body cast. I lay down on this plastic baggie that's filled with a chemical. The tech injects a different chemical into the bag. That's when things start to happen quickly. The bag starts to inflate around my back, from my tailbone up to my shoulders. After a few minutes, the stuff inside the bag hardens, and that's it, a custom fitted mold. Finally, I need to have the tattoos done. I seem to be one of the dwindling number of humans that do not have any body art, so in a strange way, I hope to up my cool factor with these. But alas, they're merely strategically placed dots that appear to be nothing more than tiny freckles.

About a week after the setup is completed, I begin my treatments. It's like having a new job. Every day, I get up in the morning, shower, get casually dressed, and drive one hour to the hospital. I take the elevator to the basement, check in with the receptionist, and head to the changing room, where I remove my shirt and don a smart looking blue hospital gown top. Then I walk down to the waiting area just outside the radiation room. My wait most mornings is just a few minutes, long enough to bury myself in the cancer survivor magazines that are cluttered on the small table next to the two marginally comfortable chairs. Just as I'm getting to the good parts about the importance of nutrition or exercise, the nurse/technician usually comes and gets me for the treatment.

The tech walks me around a long corner corridor, which leads to a huge, thick set of double doors almost like those leading to a vault in a bank. At the push of a well-placed button, the doors automatically open inward, almost invitingly. As soon as I start to walk through those doors, I see it again—the big, ominous "Radioactive" sign with the word "DANGER" prominently displayed. I guess it's important to let the patient know that you shouldn't be too close to this area . . . right before they shoot you with it from several inches away. No kidding.

The machine sits in the middle of the room and looks none too menacing. I kind of hoped for a contraption that simulated some sort of weapon, maybe like the laser beam they used to try and saw Sean Connery in half in that old James Bond movie. But it really looks more like an x-ray machine on steroids.

Speaking of lasers, they are there in the ceiling, and they're already turned on. They're shooting pinpoint beams of red light at the table jutting out from the back end of the machine. My custom fitted body mold is already situated on the table, my name written on the top in black magic marker (for those of you of a younger age, that's a Sharpie). The techs have me remove my top and lay down in the mold, then they begin a series of alignments between the machine and me. The lasers focus on my new tattoos, the table rises and tilts, finally sliding backward toward what I assume is the "gun." The techs are exceedingly nice, even asking me what kind of music I'd like to listen to during the treatment. It seems like the radiation oncology version of a blindfold and cigarette.

When everything is set and checked, the techs explain that there'll be a series of four shots to my abdomen, one each from the top, bottom, and both sides. Each shot will be about seven seconds. There will be no pain. In fact, I will feel nothing at all. Just lie still, breathe normally, and relax. Then, of course, they leave the room for the safety of the firing chamber.

The machine starts and soon after, the x-ray head is hovering over my belly. I hear a slight humming for several seconds, then the head starts to rotate to the left, stopping when it's perpendicular to my abs. "Fire two," I say to myself in my best tank commander voice. Two more shots and it's over. The techs tell me over the intercom that we're done and they'll be right in.

The whole process takes a couple of minutes at most, and not more than a total of 15 from the time I first arrived and checked in at the receptionist desk. The techs give me my appointment card for the next day, honoring my request for late mornings so I can avoid the rush hour traffic. I change back into my polo shirt and wave goodbye to the receptionist on my way out. It really is a piece of cake. Compared to getting chemotherapy, this almost feels like no therapy at all.

One down, 27 to go. God, I hope it works.

Uh Oh...

And so it goes, day after day, week after week. The only interruptions are the weekends, and the only change to the routine is the once-a-week chemo session, which is coordinated with the radiation every Tuesday. The chemo is much easier this time around since I'm only receiving one drug (Gemcytabine) during the drip. Just as with my previous therapies, my body is holding up extremely well. My appetite remains strong, my energy levels are good, no sores, no rashes, no fevers, and my nuclear resistant head of thick hair remains thick *and* on my head during the course of the treatments. Friends and family continue to marvel at how well I'm doing. When they come to visit, it takes a while for them to reconcile their expectations of what they thought I would look like with my actual appearance. That makes me smile, but deep down who knows if it matters all that much.

After three weeks, at about the halfway point in the schedule, the anticipated side effects hit me like a bus. Whereas before I was hopping and skipping to the treatments, now I am almost unable to get out of bed. What I am experiencing is an intense level of fatigue that almost defies description. It's almost like having the flu but without those pesky "flu-like" symptoms. It's almost like having the worst hangover possible, but without the hazy, semi-pleasant memories of the night before. In actuality, it's much, much worse than those. The weakness is emanating from deep within my body, and from everywhere. There's no one spot that hurts, no one area to work on. It's a full-on assault, all over, all the time.

I don't comprehend how it's happening, but I do know that I'm now in a different phase. I don't have any cuts or bruises, but my body is getting the crap beat out of it. And every day it seems to get a little bit worse. All I can do now is wake up in the morning, drag myself to the treatment, and summon the energy to get home. Other than that, I'm lying down on the couch or sleeping the rest of the hours in the day.

Eighteen down, ten to go. God, is this working?

Help Wanted

My inability to contribute to the running of the household is starting to take a huge toll on Linda. Even with Amanda helping with the kids and other tasks, things are fairly frantic. Now I know that if you ask just about any parents of two young children, you'd probably get the same assessment, but my decreasing abilities are truly affecting that delicate balance between controlled chaos and total mayhem.

Help arrives in the form of Linda's mom, Helen. She flies in from Colorado, leaving Linda's 80-year-old dad, Bill, to fend for himself for a while. We're appreciative of their sacrifice, and the truth is we really need her help. Helen is a fit 70, and a joy to have around. She's from the generation of doers and her ability to run a household is second to none. She helps with the kids, the laundry, and particularly the meals. None of this waiting until five in the afternoon to decide what's for dinner. She's planning the meal from the minute she gets up in the morning, taking out frozen items to defrost and starting prep work well in advance. Her baking and bread making often fill the air with wonderful smells that have previously been absent in the Brown house.

This help with the cooking is critical because in case I haven't mentioned it before, Linda doesn't cook. At all. It's not that she can't cook, because she's actually one heck of a baker. It's that she has zero interest in it. And zero interest translates into zero attention during the cooking process. And zero attention during the cooking process leads to just plain awful food. She has prepared about five meals in all of our years together. Okay, maybe it's ten. Really. Thankfully, I love to cook, and am actually pretty darn good at it. But right now cooking is out. As is just standing up, walking around, and many of the other mundane activities of daily living.

Thanks to Helen, we all continue to eat.

Definitions

When I was first diagnosed some months back, I swore that I would continue on with my life as normally as possible. I vowed that this disease would not define who I am. I would continue to work, live, love, and laugh.

Well, I'm wrong again. And this time it's a difficult one to swallow. The fact of the matter is that everything has changed. True, I continue to live, but my ability to work, love, and laugh has been severely damaged. What's so difficult is that the entire scope of my life is quickly being reduced. Cooking and entertaining friends? No way, I'm asleep by eight. Running around and playing with the kids in the yard? Not even close to that energy level. Hopping in the car to run some simple errands? Too tired. Taking care of important business matters? No job. Having a night out with Linda? We try, but the dark cloud hovering over our lives robs us of the true pleasure that a great date night often provides. And on it goes. The vibrancy and pleasantries of daily life replaced with doctor appointments, tests, scans, therapy sessions, and sleep. Lots and lots of sleep.

I rapidly find that all of the conversations I have begin with "How are you feeling?" and descend into the obligatory recap of what's happening on the battlefront. Don't get me wrong, I'm appreciative of the never-ending procession of calls, but it's so repetitive and draining. The conversations all center on my illness—how I'm holding up, what's next in treatment, what the doctors say, concern and sympathy. We talk about the kids and Linda of course, but always in the context of how everyone is coping with my illness. No talking about my recent trip to the coast for the trade show. No descriptions of that great risotto dish we had last night at Café Emilia. Where there used to be a steady diet of digs between my friend Ken and me about the Yankees and Mets, now there are just a few courteous, even respectful comments exchanged about our beloved teams. My return calls to friends and family are now spaced further and further apart.

Everyone tells me that the most important thing is to focus on fighting the cancer and getting better. It's my job now. Let all of the other things go. But by doing that, the cancer has now defined me. I am a cancer patient and very little else.

The worst aspect of having cancer is not how it consumes the cells in your body, but rather how it consumes your entire life.

Back from School

A little over a week ago, just before the radiation treatments started to get the better of me, I received an email from an old college roommate. He came across my contact information on the Bucknell alumni website and took the opportunity to reach out and see how I was doing.

My close group of friends at college were some of the best that I made during my entire life, and after four great years together, we received our diplomas and vowed to stay in close contact with each other, despite going in separate directions. And we did just that, getting together for weddings, taking a vacation together, and extending our friendships into young adulthood. But time and distance began to erode the closeness that we shared. Jobs, relationships, and just plain life led us to see less and less of each other and eventually the calls stopped as well. Every now and then I would hear something about one of them, but I hadn't really communicated with any of them for probably close to 15 years.

So getting an email from Marty was a complete surprise. He told me a little about his life in the San Francisco area and that he kept in contact with Mike yearly. At the end of his message, he asked how I was doing. Talk about a loaded question.

None of my circle of college friends could have had any idea what I was going through. And now, after all this time, it seems cruel that one is trying to reestablish contact and I have to ruin the fun by informing him about my cancer. I want to tell him about the great things that make up my life, how neither my sense of humor nor my sense of adventure has left me. I dream of getting together and hoisting a few for old time's sake. I can't wait to hear more stories about the gang, which he seems to still know so well. Instead, I give him a cursory recap of the recent past, which is quickly becoming the distant past. Then I tell him straight out that I have been diagnosed with inoperable pancreatic cancer. Treatments are being done and the prognosis is a difficult one.

Marty calls me within the hour of my sending that email and, after a few minutes, it is as if we spent the past 15 years talking every day. Everything comes back so easily—the joking, the banter, and most of all, the genuine caring for each other. We talk about our families and our jobs. I tell him about Linda and my two kids. After being part of my first wedding, he doesn't even know my current family. We speak at length about my illness.

Then he tells me that he is coming to the east coast next week and would love to get together. I am surprised at the coincidence, but say sure. We agree that he will come to my house that Saturday.

At two in the afternoon that Saturday, our doorbell rings, and I open the door into my past. Marty looks exactly as I expect, still with a full head of slightly graying hair, thin, and athletic. He has a huge smile and gives me a giant bear hug. Then I notice that my other roommate, Mike, is standing about 10 feet behind him. Mike lives in Ocean City, NJ, and when Marty told him about coming to see me, Mike insisted on coming along. An hour later, while we are shooting the breeze in the kitchen, the doorbell rings again, this time revealing another roommate, Jeff, and his wife, Ginny, who drove from Philadelphia to see me.

They all stay well into the night for an impromptu cookout and dinner party. We tell all of the old stories, look at pictures I keep in an old shoebox, and just laugh and laugh. Linda loves them all and they return those feelings right back to her and the kids.

A week ago, we hadn't spoken for over a decade, and now they have come to my rescue. I go to bed that night feeling better than any day since my diagnosis.

Time and distance cannot separate true friends.

It Gives Me Fever

This week's treatments seem easier. The visit from the old college roomies definitely boosted my energy level, and my meeting with Dr. F-A this week is a good one. He says the final three visits next week will be "coned down" treatments, meaning that the radiation gun will be set to a smaller, more focused field of attack. I picture pinpoint bursts of invisible magic blasting right into the heart of my tumor. It is really kind of cool how this works. It is working, right?

After my session on Friday is over, I have just three treatments left and the finish line is in sight. I'm excited to complete this phase and to regain my overall strength, which I'll need for our upcoming family trip to Walt Disney World. In fact, I'm so excited that it's giving me the chills.

The chills last well into the evening and by the next day they are joined by aches, pain, and a moderate fever. Linda urges me to go to the emergency room at our local hospital. It's Saturday, and I know that if I go to the ER, I'm going to be there for a long time. I tell her no, and we proceed to get into a huge fight.

She yells, "You're not taking this seriously!"

"It's a little fever; let's just see where it goes," I respond.

"You're being an idiot!" She storms out of the room.

My dad, brothers, and I have a long history of self-diagnosis and, as our own Dr. Browns, we decided when we were sick enough to go to the doctor, let alone the *hospital*. I do not need to go to the hospital!

Ten minutes later, a pain in the center of my chest makes it nearly impossible to breathe and knocks me to my knees. Ten minutes after that, Linda is driving us to our local hospital, Somerset Medical Center.

After another lengthy stay in the ER, complete with a multitude of blood tests, x-rays and EKGs, I'm admitted to the hospital.

"See? I told you that I needed to get here."

Linda punches me in the upper arm. Not too hard, but hard enough to let me know, "Watch it, Buster."

The stent in my bile duct has become clogged and infected again. I should know the signs by now. I get to see Dr. Serious, the GI doctor who first treated me when I became ill, and he tells me that his partner will replace my stent in the morning.

"Liquid diet today, nothing after midnight," he says with empathy. I'm already looking forward to seeing my food service friend.

Dr. S is glad to hear that other than that, I'm doing pretty well. We talk about the treatment program I'm on, and what may happen going forward. Unfortunately, he doesn't sound too optimistic about my chances. When I get to the part about the radiation and chemo shrinking the tumor down to operable status, he gets that glazed-over look in his eyes. He totally gets the strategy; he just doesn't really believe it will work.

Just once, I'd love for a doctor to go out on a limb and give me a little hope. Why can't they look beyond the science and understand that we, as patients, need it? Is it the threat of malpractice? Is it a near-fanatical sense of being weighed down by the statistics? It can't be a lack of compassion, can it? Do they worry about giving false hope? I just don't get it, but in the end, medical doctors aren't in the business of giving hope.

When it comes to that, you're on your own.

This is the second time in five months I have had the stent replaced so I'm not at all worried about the procedure. In fact, the only uncomfortable part is the last-minute prep, which happens on the operating table. You have to lie flat on your stomach, arms at your sides, and turn your head far to the right, no pillow, no resting on your forearms. The nurses then clamp a contraption around your head that has a mouthpiece that allows the tube with the instrument cluster to be inserted cleanly into your mouth and down your throat. Although they don't actually insert the darn thing until after you're out, it's still a pretty strange feeling. I watch the nurse and the doctor going through their last-minute checks when the anesthesiologist tells me that we're starting. Then, just like before, the next thing I know is that I'm waking up in the recovery room.

It's a piece of cake, which is exactly what I'm craving when I come to.

"Oh, Mr. Food Service Guy!" I shout out the door into the hallway.

None to Go

I meet with Dr. F-A to discuss the status of my treatment and whether I'm strong enough to finish the final three sessions. If I don't complete them quickly, we will eliminate them from the program. I'm not happy about that prospect at all.

"I'm good to go, let's finish this now," I tell him with a confident look that tells him that I didn't come all this way to stop short of the finish line.

He looks me over slowly. No smile, no emotion.

"Okay, start back up on Monday."

The final sessions are virtually the same as the first 25, the only difference being a slightly longer setup before the trigger gets pulled. I get through them, still driving myself to and from the hospital.

That night at home, after the final treatment, Linda and I celebrate with a nice dinner and a glass of wine. I'm proud of the accomplishment, but so worried about the outcome. It's now the middle of summer, six months since my symptoms first appeared and my journey began. Since the radiation continues to work after the final treatment, I've been told to wait about a month, then have my scans taken. I schedule them for the day before we're leaving for Florida and set up an appointment with the surgeon for the day after we return. I sure hope the "happiest place on earth" can keep my mind from going crazy with panic during those two weeks.

I am physically spent from this round of treatment. The simultaneous chemo and radiation, compounded by the surgical procedure and hospital stay, has left me mostly bedridden. I have so little energy; I spend most of the days sleeping, which unfortunately means that I'm often awake during the nights.

One of the toughest challenges that I'm facing is the ability to mentally cope with the disease. It's the first thing that I think of when I wake up, and it's the last thing that I think about before I fall asleep. During the days, it helps that there are some distractions to help push the worry into the background. It doesn't really disappear, but it does move back from front and center. But in the middle of the night, it's just me and Mr. Worry. The family is sleeping soundly (my youngsters are real pros at sleeping through the night in their own beds) and I'm alone. I used to love this quiet time, as well as the early mornings, before everyone else woke up. Now I dread it. I usually can't go back to sleep, so I resort to watching TV. It doesn't really help, as I still find myself overwhelmed with thoughts of tumors, odds, prayers, and death. Maybe there's an infomercial product out there with a market for people like me.

Sometimes I take a sleeping pill to get me through the night, but most of the time, I just lay there thinking.

Twenty-eight down, none to go. God, I hope this worked.

Strangers and a Friend

The weeks following my treatments are filled with lots of rest and anticipation. It's a busy time in the Brown household, preparing for our pilgrimage to Disney and all. Unfortunately, I'm not able to contribute all that much. Linda and Amanda continue to piece together the necessities for our trip, and I work on getting strong enough to make it at all. We're all very excited and it helps tremendously by taking some of the focus away from the pending tests.

I do start to recover as the weeks go by, gradually regaining some level of strength and energy. Maybe they won't need to wheel me around after all. Mentally, I concentrate a lot on the vacation, and try hard to give myself a break from the daily stress.

But then, a news headline:

'Last Lecture' Professor Randy Pausch Dies at 47.

The news hits me very hard. Although I have been following his journey closely, I'm not prepared for the hurt it brings. I knew that his prognosis was terminal, but somehow I held on to a fantasy that he would survive. I wanted someone to look up to, to keep my hopes alive. Randy Pausch was so visible, and so good for the pancreatic cancer cause. I'm afraid that his loss will only be visible to his core followers. To everyone else, he and our cause will quickly fade. Why couldn't he have lived?

Maybe Patrick Swayze will. Patrick was diagnosed earlier this year, about a month or so before I was. He was also inoperable, but underwent some sort of "procedure," the details of which were hard to come by. I mean, with his kind of money, he's got to be able to get the latest, most experimental kind of treatment available. It's believed that he underwent CyberKnife®

treatment, a "bladeless surgery" that uses ultra-intense pinpoint radiation to attack an otherwise-inoperable tumor. Stanford Medical Center invented the technology over 20 years ago and has been using it on inoperable pancreatic tumors for several years with some promising results. But seeing Patrick's pictures in the tabloids, it doesn't look like it's working.

On a much more personal level, a colleague of mine is going through the PC journey at this same time. Lanny and I met when I was the president of the art materials company, and he was the vice president for one of our biggest customers. Through our business, we developed a relationship characterized by deep respect for each other.

He was diagnosed in late 2007, just a few months before me. I remember thinking that he was in deep trouble. He immediately underwent surgery to remove the tumor and began follow-up chemotherapy after he sufficiently recovered from the operation. He was private in his battle, with irregular updates about his condition circulating among colleagues in the industry every now and then.

After I was diagnosed, he reached out to me and we began a regular series of calls back and forth that provided a lifeline for each of us. He was having a difficult time gaining his weight back and he still had a fair amount of pain and discomfort, but his scans were looking good. His prognosis is certainly better than mine. Since he is already down the PC road further than I am, his insights are invaluable. We're able to share our strategies for coping with side effects, which medicines are working, and what doesn't work. His good health is providing a beacon for me in my fight.

The Calm Before the Storm

The final weeks leading up to the Disney trip go by quickly, with my kids' level of excitement reaching a fever pitch. Their energy pulls me along, and by the day before we leave, I'm feeling okay. Not great, but good, serviceable.

The day before our trip is also the day for tests. I go to the diagnostic center and submit to the familiar series of CT scans and MRIs. The tests are now routine for me, but the stakes are anything but. This is the big one. This is what I've been subjecting myself to the treatments for. The CT scan is quick, but the MRI is long, noisy, and uncomfortable. I try to let myself fall into a sort of meditative trance while I'm in the tube. After 45 minutes, the techs are helping me up and I'm done. I feel good. I know the treatments have worked.

The next day, the family, including Amanda, is off to Florida for a week of sun and fun in Mickeyland. We're staying in a two-bedroom timeshare about a mile outside of the parks. We arrive, check in, and unpack our considerable amount of stuff, all with a minimum amount of trouble. Taylor and Colton are doing really well, considering the long day of travel we've been through. Such is the power of the Mouse.

We spend the next seven days visiting the parks in the mornings and coming back to the timeshare in the early afternoons when the temps hit the mid-to-high nineties. The kids nap, Linda and I recover, and Amanda keeps the routines going. By later in the day, the kids are in the pool cooling off and the grownups are sitting nearby, sipping cool drinks. Our dinners are split between home cooked meals, which I prepare at the timeshare, and casual family restaurants. Linda and Amanda are certain that we look like a blended family. Amanda appears to be my older daughter from a previous marriage, while Linda seems to be a newer, younger wife with our new young children. I can see how that would appear, and we share a few good laughs over some of the stares we get.

The week flies by, and we all have a great time. The kids are overwhelmed by the Magic Kingdom®, and every new experience brings wide-eyed amazement and smiles from them. Linda and Amanda enjoy doting on the kids and getting in their lounge time around the pool.

As for me, it just feels great to be away! I came here thinking that this was something we had to do at least once so the kids would have a memory of our family at Disney. But cooking for the family, playing in the pool with Colt and Taylor, being able to lift them up and toss them around in the water, and the days at the parks all make me feel like there's a chance for normalcy. It's a magical vacation for all of us. We're pretty much worn out by week's end, and we're ready for the trip home.

I feel mentally and physically recharged and I'm ready for the next steps: surgery, recovery, survival. It can happen; I've started to believe that it will happen.

Even for me, such is the power of the Mouse.

The Next Big Drop

The wait in Dr. Supersmart's waiting room was short, but now that we've been in the examining room for 25 minutes, I'm reaching my limit. When he walks into the room, whenever that may be, my life will change again. Either we're going forward with surgery, or we're moving on to a different, more difficult path.

Finally, there's a simultaneous knock and opening of the door, and he appears. As always, there's no emotion on his face—no smile, no frown, no nothing.

"Okay, your tumor has shrunk about 20 percent," he says, and before my lips even begin to curl up in a smile, he adds, "but not enough to be operable."

I'm stunned, but I don't collapse into a heap on the floor. Linda is stoic, hardly reacting at all, just listening intently.

"What now?" she asks.

"Well, the best bet would be more treatment. Keep working and see if we can shrink it further. It'll have to be more chemo, since you've just finished your lifetime allotment of radiation."

For the first time in our meetings, I finally understand what the heck he's saying. No medical mumbo jumbo, no $500 words. I don't like what I hear.

"Is that feasible? Can it work?" I question him, almost pleadingly.

"I have had patients who have gone through several years of treatments and then we were able to operate, so yes it can work. Your next step is to make another appointment with your oncologist."

He shakes our hands, manages a slight smile, and walks us to the exit. We close the door behind us and start down the next road in our journey.

Although I don't get the news that I was expecting, I remain surprisingly calm. Based on what my surgeon said, I'm choosing to look at the positives. The tumor did shrink, there's still no evidence that the disease has spread, and there are still treatment options. I'm still in the game.

A few days later, we're again waiting in an examination room, this time with an appointment to see Dr. Direct. We're anxious to hear what he has to say, his opinion of the modest success so far, and what treatments he has in mind to continue the assault on this pesky tumor.

He enters the room after a short wait and is pleasant as he greets Linda and me. Then he begins.

"I'm sorry that it didn't work. We need to think about which direction to go."

I'm surprised by his opening comment, but I respond, "The surgeon explained that with more chemo, there's a possibility of getting the tumor to shrink more and have surgery. In fact, he's had patients who've gone through years of treatments and became operable."

Dr. D becomes very serious and sternly informs us that he disagrees. That outcome has occurred only once or twice, and not for someone with pancreatic cancer.

"The fact is that you are still inoperable, and you need to understand that you will never become operable."

We both question why he disagreed with the surgeon.

"Because he will only see you again if you become operable. He's freer to be optimistic. As your oncologist, I'm the one in charge of your overall care and I have to be more realistic. I have to tell it like it really is," he says, looking us straight in the eyes.

"What's the next step then?" I ask through the explosions and haze that are enveloping my head.

"I don't know yet, I'll need to give that some thought. Call and make an appointment for a week from now."

We ask him his thoughts on the CyberKnife treatment, and he tells us that he knows just a little about it. He knows of some positive results, and he has referred some patients to Beth Israel Deaconess Medical Center in Boston.

Linda and I slowly rise from our chairs. We courteously shake his hand and thank him for his care. We leave the office and ride the elevator four floors down. We pass by the gorgeous atrium with the gourmet coffee stand next to the pharmacy. We nod to the security guard as we pass by the reception desk. Then we're out the doors, into our car, and turning left out of the driveway. I glance back at the hospital in the rear view mirror.

We're not coming back.

Unlike the other trips home after we received bad news, this one wasn't quiet. In fact, we're loudly recounting what just happened.

"What gives with these doctors?" Linda asks incredulously.

"I know. I can't believe that they play with you like this. One says keep trying, but his colleague basically says that that was just a bunch of crap," I counter.

The more we recap the appointment, the more frustrated we become. We just don't understand their reluctance to keep fighting. To be honest, we really like Dr. D, and feel betrayed by what's just happened.

As our immediate emotions calm down, reality and worry once again start to take over. The only real chance for a cure is gone. Who knows what this CyberKnife can do? It certainly hasn't been touted as an alternative route to a cure. I stay quiet for the rest of the ride home.

The roller coaster keeps throwing us around and my options are dwindling.

Time to Get to Work

I have a very restless sleep that night, tossing, turning, and sleeping in short bursts. I wake up again at about 7:00 and look over to see that Linda's side of the bed is empty. That's strange since it's Saturday and she loves to sleep late on her days off. She's not in the bathroom, nor in either of the kid's rooms. I walk downstairs to find her at the computer. She barely looks up at me, but starts talking in a confident voice.

"Okay, here's what I've found out. There are a lot of articles about new treatments they're performing at New York Presbyterian. Other hospitals too, but NYP seems be the place. Add in the fact that Dr. Supersmart said that one of the best PC surgeons in the country is at NYP—the one that you would need if you could ever have the surgery—and I think that's where we should go next."

It's clear that she's been researching options by herself for some time. I find myself listening intently and nodding with her conclusions. I again remember how important it is to have a support system in place. After yesterday's news, I was having a hard time functioning, but Linda stepped right up and again took over.

We're on our own now and need to decide what to do next and where to do it. We spend the day looking over websites, talking to Linda's sister, Laura, and reaching some conclusions. By the next morning, we've got a plan.

We're no longer going to put all our eggs in one basket. We cannot afford to waste time going down a single road, only to conclude that it won't work. We're going to explore multiple options simultaneously and make the best decision we can with the information available.

That night we "celebrate" our tenth anniversary with a quiet dinner at a nearby five star romantic restaurant inside a century-old boutique hotel. Earlier that evening, Linda presented me with a home movie that she made using photos and video clips from our years together. There were shots of us when we were younger (and I was thinner and healthier), on vacations, and fun times at home with our growing family, all set to our favorite music. During any normal time, the video would have been a real tearjerker, but it was so sweet and sentimental that tonight, it was almost unfair to watch. Yet I know that it won't be the only time I turn it on.

After we place our order for the five-course tasting menu with accompanying wine selections, I reach into my pocket and take out her present.

"I have a few things that I have to say to you," I begin.

"It's been a great ten years. We've been through a lot, but we also have a lot. And we have Taylor and Colton. Having kids was the best decision ever," I continue.

"Thank you for everything you've done these past six months. I know that without you and your help, I wouldn't still be here. Happy anniversary, baby."

We toast each other just as Linda starts to wipe away some tears.

"I know that my marriage proposal wasn't a surprise or very romantic. I hope this is more like it."

I hand her a stunning diamond eternity anniversary wedding band that takes her breath away. Mission accomplished.

On Monday I speak to Stanford Medical Center's CyberKnife team. They give me the information and agree to review my case as soon as I send them my medical file. It goes out to them that day. I'm excited about this prospect, as it's the next best alternative for someone like me. Hell, it was *invented* at Stanford to treat tumors that couldn't be treated with traditional surgery. There were even some cases reported on the CyberKnife treatment turning previously inoperable PC patients operable.

I also call and make an appointment with the chief PC surgeon at NYP, saying that Dr. S at Hackensack Medical Center referred me to him. Linda and I know that I need to see the oncologist there who invented a new chemotherapy cocktail, so our strategy is to get in to see the surgeon through the Hackensack referral, then get to the oncologist as a referral from the surgeon.

Maybe it's all a little sneaky, but we are playing by the rules.

And rules aside, we're running our own playbook now.

Nights Are Forever

Despite the developments of the past week, I'm holding together reasonably well.

The days are kept tolerable by the various goings on with the family. Taylor is now in first grade, so she's getting her initial taste of the longer school days. And although Colton is now pre-school age, we decide against it and keep him home with Amanda continuing as our nanny.

The nights continue to be difficult. In fact, much more difficult. I spend hour after hour horrified about my prognosis. Since I was first diagnosed, I quickly learned that there was only one way to beat this: through successful surgery. Now that possibility is dead and I need to somehow unlearn that fact. I need a new path of hope and, even though my heart is breaking, my head keeps searching for a way. By the time morning comes, I'm usually an exhausted wreck.

During the days, I continue to research the CyberKnife treatments as much as I can. There are some references to success, but nothing is written about it being a method for cure. I place my falling hopes with Stanford and create a new road to survival: CyberKnife the tumor to operability, cut the sucker out, and make history.

I know it's the longest of long shots, but I start to sleep a tiny bit better.

Before I fall asleep one night, I see a TV commercial for a different type of cancer hospital. The first thing that prompts me to sit up and stare at the screen is that the spokesperson is a young woman named Peggy, and she is a pancreatic cancer survivor. She speaks passionately about the facility, the doctors, and most importantly, how the entire experience brought a level of hope that she had not felt before. And how they saved her life.

Cancer Treatment Centers of America advertises that they treat the whole cancer patient using a comprehensive array of traditional and supplemental methods that other cancer centers simply do not use. The testimonials are compelling and they close with their signature phrase: "Winning the fight against cancer, every day®."

The next day, I visit the CTCA website and immerse myself in the hope it exudes. More importantly, there are two testimonials from stage 4 pancreatic cancer survivors. Nobody survives stage 4 PC, yet these two folks apparently have. I don't comprehend how that's possible, and I don't really care.

If they came back and survived, then maybe I can too. Maybe there is another path to survival.

Two Sentences

"Thank you for your interest in Stanford Medical Center."

"We have reviewed your medical records and have determined that you are not a candidate for CyberKnife therapy."

My last best chance obliterated in a two sentence email. No phone call, no explanation. If this was a rejection from a job interview, I'd be angrier than hell by the cowardly callousness of their response, but it's my life at stake, and my body seems to crumble under the stress. I get small, uncontrollable shakes in my arms, hands, and upper half of my torso. Thank God Linda is right there with me. In fact, she read the message first and asked me to come upstairs to the bedroom, trying to soften the blow as she delivered the news.

"I can't believe Stanford turned me down," I cry to Linda.

The walls aren't just closing in now; they're falling down on top of us from all sides.

"I can't believe it, no one can help us?" I add, losing it completely.

Our Kind of Town?

As you can guess, Linda had already absorbed the news and gotten to work adding new pages to the playbook. She had already spoken to our oncologist at Hackensack and asked for the information about the CyberKnife team at Boston Beth Israel Deaconess Medical Center. It helps that there's already another option in place, but I'm not optimistic that their opinion will differ from Stanford. I call Deaconess that day and they come through right away, setting up an appointment for the following week. The appointment with the surgeon at NYP is a few days after that. We're improvising like hell now and throwing a lot at the walls. Something has got to stick, right? Once again, we've created a new road where there wasn't one before.

It's a sunny, cool day when Linda and I head up to Boston to see the team at Beth Israel Deaconess Medical Center. It's a little over four hours by car and we hit very little traffic. We arrive at the medical campus and head for the bowels of the building where the "bladeless surgical magic" happens. Why do my appointments always seem to be in the basement?

Dr. Possibility and his team have been performing CyberKnife treatments on inoperable pancreatic tumors for a couple of years now. Apparently, the treatments have been showing some promise in cases just like mine. They certainly have not established the CyberKnife as a curative process, but they are encouraged by the length of time the treatment is adding to patients' lives. They have several patients who are still alive 18 months post-treatment. As for making tumors operable, it becomes a whole lot more cloudy. Yes, it has happened, but obviously, there's no real history of how these patients have fared. It's too new.

I undergo the usual exam room interview, then it's off to the CT scan so they have their own picture of what's going on in my pancreas. The doctor is confident that he can help me. What that exactly means is left open to my own interpretation. We set up an appointment for the end of the following week, as this will give them the proper time to review my scans and prepare the treatment program. We leave the appointment with a mixed set of emotions. On one hand, CyberKnife here at Deaconess seems to be a promising new course of treatment and, most importantly, they will treat me. But it doesn't appear to be the magical cure I had been fantasizing about. Reality stinks.

As we're leaving the hospital, Linda surprises me with tickets to the Red Sox home playoff game that night vs. the Tampa Bay Devil Rays at Fenway. While I was in with the CT technicians, she was on the phone with a ticket broker.

"Let's stay over, see the game, and enjoy the city. Boston's a great place, it'll be fun."

I agree with everything she says, except the part about a Red Sox playoff game being fun. I can't root against them and expect to get out of there alive, and I certainly won't root for them. But I'm not above making a pact with the Red Sox devil. You know, I'll root for your team, and maybe you can pull some strings with the CyberKnife gods. I'm too far gone to realize what a lunatic I've become. We get a hotel room, check in, and head to a sports store to pick up some nighttime attire for the game. It's pretty chilly in Boston in October. Despite the surprising variety of Yankees gear at this place, the store clerk strongly recommends that we not wear any to Fenway that night. So we buy some generic windbreakers and the like, then I do something that clearly shows the state of delirium that I'm in—I buy and wear a Red Sox hat to the game. Despite my New Yawk accent, I totally "blend" at Fenway. Our seats are 20 rows behind home plate with a perfect view of the Green Monster. It turns out to be a great game, with the Sox coming from way behind to beat the Rays. Woohoo! We leave early and walk back to the hotel, hearing roars from the stadium every few blocks. I have to admit, what a great atmosphere. What a *normal* night. We get to the hotel and share a late night toast, "Here's to Boston."

All I Need is a Hero

Linda's position as a global human resources director requires her to travel internationally. She regularly visits India, China, and Argentina to oversee service centers, and while she has usually been able to alter her schedule to accommodate my endless doctor visits, this week is different. Important meetings in Buenos Aires require her presence, thus I'll be visiting NYP alone.

New York Presbyterian Hospital/Columbia University Medical Center is consistently ranked as the top hospital in New York, and one of the top ten in the country. Despite those lofty credentials, in my 50 years on this earth, I have never stepped foot into the place.

It's been a little over a month since I received the news that I would not be able to have surgery, and since then, almost everything has continued in a steady downward spiral. I've become quiet, sad, and desperate as I realize that the statistics probably don't lie. Keeping my hope up is the toughest challenge and I know in my heart that as my options dry up, so too will my hope.

As I approach the George Washington Bridge on my way to NYP, I find myself remembering the days when I was a kid and would drive into the city with my dad on his way to work. He owned a liquor store on 81st Street and Columbus Avenue, right around the corner from where he and my mom grew up. After they moved to the suburbs in New Jersey, he would make the 45 minute commute 6 days a week, 50-plus weeks a year. For some reason, one of my most vivid memories was paying the toll. Back in the sixties, you either had to pay with cash or the discount trip book. My dad always had the 30 day book and he'd keep it tucked tightly in his sun visor. Then, methodically, he would pull it out, slide one ticket between his thumb and forefinger, partially tear it to give a head start, and flip his wrist to expose the ticket to the tollbooth attendant. They always exchanged a quick hello, and we were back on our way. It was probably one of the more mundane things he would do each day, but I always thought it was so cool and I couldn't wait to be old enough to drive so I could "flip my wrist" and pay the toll.

As I approach the toll today, after sitting in traffic for 30 minutes, the ticket books are long gone, as is the dollar toll. Heck, there are hardly attendants anymore, having being replaced by E-ZPass® scanners and cameras. The eight bucks come off my account automatically as I zip through the toll plaza at twenty-five mph, or about ten over the suggested speed limit. I look out over the Manhattan skyline and marvel at the beauty of it, despite the gaping hole left at ground zero. I exit at Riverside Drive, make a couple of quick turns, and I'm in the parking lot handing over my keys to a surprisingly pleasant parking lot valet.

I enter the Herbert Irving Comprehensive Cancer Center, take the elevator up to the eighth floor, and check in at the gastrointestinal cancer reception desk.

I have an appointment with Dr. J. Hero, one of the country's leading pancreatic cancer surgeons. Although I know I'm not a candidate for surgery, I hope that he can take a fresh look at my records and point me in a new direction. I know that it's grasping at straws, but what else do I have left? After a relatively short wait, his nurse practitioner calls me in and performs a lengthy interview, rehashing the last eight months of this nightmare.

After about 45 minutes of note taking, she gets up and leaves the room, re-entering a few minutes later.

"He's ready to see you now," she says while walking me down the hall to his office.

When I enter, I'm surprised at its small size, but I guess the operating room is his true domain. He introduces himself, as well as one of his associates who's sitting in on the consultation.

Dr. Hero is about my age with a slight build and short, dark hair. His handshake is firm and warm. He lets me begin with a short introduction about myself and the journey that has brought me here today. I clarify my goals with him as he listens intently.

Then he starts to speak, and his first words change everything.

"I've reviewed the MRI and CT scans you sent to me and compared them to the written report from your medical team. There seems to be a discrepancy."

So Close

I have no idea what he is talking about, and only in my wildest dreams did I ever envision his next sentence.

"The report from Dr. Optimism says that there is no margin around the tumor for it to be surgically removed, but looking at the scans, it's clear to me that you are, in fact, operable."

"Stunned" is much too small a word to describe what I feel at this moment, as everything I've been shooting for has just materialized. I hold it together and ask him how that can be.

He replies, "There are some caveats that need to be explained. Firstly, I greatly respect Dr. O's work, and we've worked together many times. He was inside of you with the scope, and if he determined that the tumor is still too wrapped around the artery, then I would tend to believe him over the scans."

He offers to show me the scans and turns his computer screen slightly to reveal them. He scrolls through several images and starts to point out where my pancreas and artery are. Then, for the first time, I see the villain itself in all of its black and gray glory. I have to admit that I'm struggling to see what he's pointing out until he switches to the same shot taken three months earlier. Now, with his verbal cues, the change practically jumps off the screen at me. Whereas my scans from May showed the tumor intimately involved with the artery, these latest scans clearly show an area of space between the two. Even I can see it.

"Mr. Brown, you know that even with this development, it's unfortunately well past the time frame in which we operate."

Again, I haven't a clue what he's talking about.

"We only perform surgery within a short window of no more than six weeks post-radiation. You're already at eleven weeks today. It's too late to operate. Certainly your medical team told you this."

He seems genuinely surprised and saddened when I inform him that they had not.

He enlightens me about how the radiation has continued to blast away at my insides well past the final treatment. In addition to battling the tumor, it also weakens all of the good tissue in the surrounding areas. It's this good tissue that is needed to reconnect all of the plumbing during the Whipple surgery. At eleven weeks, there's no way of knowing how far the radiation has gone, no way of knowing if there's enough good tissue left to survive the many connections.

Once again, my head is exploding, and I'm not even sure that I'm hearing all of this correctly. How could I have come here by myself? Why did Linda have to be in Argentina now?

After a long wait, I ask him what my options are.

"Based upon what I see and read, I believe that your best option is to see one of my colleagues in oncology. You clearly need systemic therapy and he's developed a lot of new chemotherapy cocktails that are having a positive impact on patients like yourself."

I stare at him for a long time, then glance over to his associate, and finally back to Dr. Hero.

"They don't provide a cure, do they," I say with a tone that's more statement than question.

"No, Mr. Brown, they do not. I believe that you can expect a short period of decent health, then there will be a rapid and definitive decline."

The cruel irony of this is beyond my comprehension. The treatments actually worked and we didn't find out until it was too late? This cannot be happening. But it is.

Dr. H lets me take all of this in slowly. He's a compassionate man and he knows what's going through my head. He's seen this pain all too many times before.

I thank them for their time and slowly get up from the chair. I feel like I need some help to make it out. As I turn toward the door, I can't help but realize that it's game over.

The Magic Moment

Until now, I hoped to find a doctor who shared my optimistic fantasies of beating this, a doctor who was not jaded by the stark reality of the fight.

Until now, I have been the good soldier, dutifully following the course of action prescribed by the experts. Sure, Linda and I have been aggressive in searching for information and answers, but we have never strayed from the direction given by the doctors.

But now, in the few seconds it takes to reach the door, my brain explodes into overdrive, bombarding me with thoughts and images. I see those damn scans, my deceased parents, a hospital bed, and Linda and the kids alone. I can't process it all and I'm certain that I'm going to pass out. Then, as I reach for the doorknob, something happens. Everything in my head becomes quiet and I stop.

Everyone has heard that when a person is faced with a life threatening situation, the fight-or-flight reaction takes over. In that moment, your body surges with adrenaline as you make a decision to run or fight. This is my moment. Walk through that door and face certain death, or take a stand and fight. My hand stops before it reaches the doorknob.

Standing up straighter, I turn back around.

"With all due respect, Doctor, I cannot accept this. I can't leave here not knowing if I can have that surgery. This is my life at stake."

I walk back over to the desk and stand behind the chair I was just sitting in.

"I need to know. I cannot go home and start checking days off of the calendar as I wait to die. What if we did the endoscopic test again and it showed that there was adequate margin around the tumor. Would you operate on me?"

He glances over at his colleague, then back at me.

"You seem like an intelligent guy, you know what you're up against. There are many complications, but I agree. You deserve to know."

He adds, "We have no time to waste, let's schedule the test for tomorrow, and we'll do it here. If it shows the proper margins and you're willing to assume the enormous risk, then yes, I'll operate on you."

Finally, an honest to goodness hero has joined the team.

Not Just Co-Workers

I don't know if this new take-charge attitude will deliver me to the promised land of medical cure, but I have just learned a critical lesson.

You are your own best advocate. Above all others, it's you who must look out for yourself. Listen to what the doctors say, but don't believe everything they say as the gospel. Just like us, they are products of their skills and experiences. What one doctor says is not what another will say. What one surgeon believes is possible is not the same as what another may be capable of doing. Keep searching, keep believing. Never, ever give up.

I feel re-energized as I walk the long city block back to the parking lot to retrieve my car. Never has the roller coaster been more in motion than in the past couple of hours. From anticipation and hope, to bewilderment and despair, and back again to hope.

As I pass back over the GW to New Jersey, I speed dial Linda's cell phone. She's in the middle of dawn-till-dusk meetings, but she's been nervously awaiting my call. I hear clicks and buzzes as the call transfers to some cell tower in Argentina.

Finally she answers, "Hold on a second."

It's actually more like 30 seconds before she comes back on.

"Okay, I had to excuse myself from a meeting with a roomful of people; I'm out in the hallway. How'd it go?"

I bring her up to date and add that I've already spoken to Amanda. We're working on a plan to get a substitute babysitter so she can accompany me to the test tomorrow. I'll need someone to drive me home after I wake up from the anesthesia.

Linda's reaction to all of this is pure fury—fury at the doctors for not telling us the time limits and fury at the fact that she's more than 5,000 miles away. Her mind shifts into high gear as she tells me that she's going to figure out a way to be here for the test, which is now less than 24 hours away.

Linda's boss, Michael, and co-workers stop their meeting and spend the next few hours figuring out the logistics of getting her to New York City by 10 a.m. the following morning. Flights are booked, drivers are arranged, and before you can say "High Performance, Delivered," she's on her way back to her hotel to pack, check out, and get to the airport for the all-night flight back to the states.

Her colleagues at Accenture are proving to be not just co-workers, but friends who come through when the needs are great.

In the Nick of Time

The next morning arrives quickly after a surprisingly restful night. I was on the phone with my brothers and friends well past 11:00 bringing everyone up to speed with the latest and greatest in my saga. I fell asleep quickly and didn't wake up until 6:00.

Amanda and her brother, Nick, arrive bright and early, even before the kids are awake. Nick is a couple of years older than his sister and looks every bit the part of a "Jersey Shore" cast member. His hair is perfectly coifed and spiked about three inches high and every aspect of his appearance is perfectly groomed. It's a welcome change from the standard grunge look that so many of his peers sport these days. I've met him a couple of times before and he's a good guy. Linda and I are completely comfortable with him watching Taylor and Colton. Amanda has already briefed him on the basics and, after I thank him for coming through for us on such short notice, she and I are off to NYP.

We arrive and check in at the reception desk on the endoscopy floor. I'm very focused on the procedure that's ahead and, thankfully, Amanda is not too chatty. The appointment is scheduled for 10:00 and, as is par for the course, they're running late. That's a good thing today, since it gives us a little more time for Linda to arrive. Her plane landed at LaGuardia Airport a little over 40 minutes ago, and she's en route to the hospital right now. She and Amanda are texting like crazy on their cell phones while I'm entrenched in the morning news shows on the small flat screen TV.

A little past 10:30, Linda steps out of the elevator and into the reception area. She looks pretty darn good considering the hectic last minute travel. Maybe even better than me. After a long hug, we join Amanda back on the couch and wait to be called in for the test.

That call comes quickly, and after changing into the standard hospital procedure garb and getting an IV inserted into my arm, Dr. Bignews arrives. He explains that he's spoken with Dr. Hero and understands my case and the objective of today's test, assuring us that he'll take as much time as needed to reach a definitive conclusion. In a short while, we'll know one way or the other.

Can it Be?

It's been about 30 minutes since I've been back in the reception area. The scoping of my pancreas was completed a little over 90 minutes ago, and after the obligatory stint in recovery while the anesthesia wore off, Linda and I are now back on that same couch with Amanda waiting for the results. Since Dr. B is not yet finished with another procedure he started while I was still out, we just sit and wait. It's been more than nine months since my symptoms first appeared, and over seven since first hearing that terrifying diagnosis. Another 30 minutes here or there isn't such a big deal. Is it?

We're now into the middle of the afternoon and the sun is shining brightly through the tall windows behind our couch. It casts a glare onto the TV, making it difficult for me to watch the news. Patients continue to come and go while the receptionist methodically calls them up to the desk for processing. I can't help but wonder if any of them are waiting for life and death results like I am.

Finally, and without warning, the doctor appears, expressionless, and approaches us directly.

"You definitely have available margins. I've already spoken to Dr. Hero. He's in surgery now, but he'll be calling you by early evening."

"So you're saying that I'm operable? For sure?" I ask one more time to be certain.

"Yes, I'm sure," he says, finally smiling just a little bit.

Tears are welling up in my eyes and I tell him that I want to hug him. It seems to surprise him. Instead I turn to Linda and we bury our faces in each other's shoulders.

The three of us are standing in the middle of the reception area surrounded by 20-or-so other patients who are glancing up to watch us. Amanda is still over by the couch, but she can tell what's happening.

The tears are rolling down my cheeks now as I shake his hand and thank him again and again. Just before he turns to walk away, I wrap my arms around him and tell him one last thank you. He seems a little embarrassed, but he understands. He smiles and wishes us good luck.

That, ladies and gentleman, is what we refer to as another miracle.

You Ought to Be in Pictures

Dr. Hero meets with us on Monday morning, the first available appointment since my test on Friday. He really isn't wasting any time.

"As I've said, there are many complications in your case, and that increases the risks significantly. But you are operable, and that gives us a chance for the home run, a cure. Do you want to have the surgery?"

Linda and I discussed this over the weekend and it didn't take long. We didn't need to talk with anyone else. We didn't need to list the pros and cons. I had been scanned, poked, chemo'd, and radiated, all for the chance of getting to this point.

"Doctor, this is an easy decision. We're going for the surgery," I respond while holding Linda's hand in mine.

"Good, I've taken the liberty of booking an operating room for this Friday. It was the first available opening and I didn't want to wait any longer. It will have been 13 weeks by that time."

We talk about the difficulties involved in the surgery, how he's not certain how far the radiation effect has traveled. His plan is to go as far as necessary to find good tissue to reconnect, even if it means removing more of my organs than normal. He excuses himself for a minute, leaving us alone with his assistant. We exchange some small talk about the surgery, going over what to expect in broad terms.

"Please excuse me for that interruption, but there's a production crew from ABC news here today," he says, somewhat embarrassed.

He discloses that they are doing a story on Patrick Swayze and his battle with PC, and that they are interviewing him as part of the segment.

"Let me ask you both something. If they are interested, would you mind being interviewed? They are considering filming part of a Whipple surgery."

We're both more than a little surprised by the request, but flattered that he thought highly enough of us to make that suggestion to the ABC people.

When he returns, he has a release form for each of us to sign. Not exactly the scenario you dream of when you picture yourself on TV, but it's a pleasant diversion during an unsettling and scary meeting. We thank him for his time and commitment and remind him to get plenty of rest this week.

We leave the office with a growing sense of optimism and a lively bounce in our step.

Golden Child

"Well, that was pretty amazing. ABC news is using our doctor for the TV show. I guess we've got the right guy," I comment to Linda as we wait for the parking valet to bring our car, "and they may want to film my surgery too!"

"You're a Golden Child," she says to me with a big smile.

Linda has called me that a few times during our time together. She uses it to describe this aura that she believes is surrounding me.

"There's an energy that is always working in your favor, always looking out for you," she asserts, "and this time is no different."

I have to admit that while a certain part of that seems true, much of it relates to my career and the choices I've made along the way. Several times I've walked away from solid jobs and career paths to try my hand at establishing myself elsewhere.

I walked away from a promising accounting career at a Big 8 accounting firm to take a position as a human resource manager with a competing company. I essentially walked away from all of my educational and practical training. My friends and family, especially my father, thought I was nuts. A year and a half later, I was back in corporate financial management as controller/CFO of an emerging olive oil company. My foray into H.R. hadn't derailed me a bit. In fact, I learned a lot about managing and motivating people, which is essential to being a successful manager. That company went on to become one of the true success stories of the eighties and nineties and I grew right along with it. There was wonderful international travel, prestige, and endless rewards. The golden child had been born.

At the height of that successful run, I resigned to become a VP of a tiny Italian foods company, which was one-twentieth the size of my previous employer. I left for the money, and I left to help rebuild something new. The company was a shell of its own prior glory and, after only one year, it was still hanging on by less than a thread. The fire consumed many of the employees around me, but somehow I rose out of it and was offered the position of president. The company was all but dead, but hadn't yet received its official certificate. It couldn't survive, yet I was being given the chance to stay and change my career forever, moving from the financial floor to the executive suite. I took the job, stayed three years, and grew the business more than fivefold. Overall, it turned out not to be a bad decision, it worked out well. The golden child was growing.

That energy seems to extend to my life outside of the business world as well. Although I certainly experienced my fair share of challenges, disappointments, and tragedies (my father dying at a young age, my first marriage ending in divorce, my mother suffering a long, debilitating illness that took her life as well), the overall karma in my life is almost always positive.

Linda often points out that within my large group of friends and acquaintances, I am extremely well liked and respected and am rarely, if ever, involved in the drama that goes on within those circles. Furthermore, I'm one of the only people who can say what needs to be said, good or bad, and not be crucified or excommunicated for it. I think it's because I'm a good friend who's available and honest. She thinks it's more than that. She thinks it's because I'm the golden child.

As we get into the car with Linda driving and me again starting the long process of making update phone calls, I pause to think about what she just said.

I mean, it's been close to nine months now. If I look at this thing objectively, cutting out the mental strain, the fear and depression, the brutal treatments and physical side effects, there's one undeniable fact: *I am still alive.* Not just still alive, but operable, with no detectable spread of this disease that kills 75% of its victims within the first 12 months. Not just still alive, but getting ready to step up to the plate for a chance at a home run. When almost all PC patients are staring at their final days ahead, I'm four days away from the big game. Maybe there is something to this golden child thing.

We're about to find out.

July 10, 1974

We were playing one of our fiercest archrivals, Ridgefield Park, or just "The Park," as we unaffectionately called them. I turned 17 five days earlier and was enjoying my favorite passion, baseball. I was playing shortstop for the Teaneck, NJ, Connie Mack team, and we were playing them on our home field at Teaneck High School.

We played The Park several times during the season and the games drew big crowds, as they were one of the area's perennial baseball powers. I enjoyed playing them, particularly at their home field, where the games were played at night under the lights. That was a big deal in those days.

But this game was at home in the warm sun. There were lots of friends and regular townsfolk in the crowd that day and, of course, my mom. Whereas my dad rarely, if ever, attended my games due to his six-days-a-week business, my mom was at virtually every game I played since I started Little League at age nine. She was very involved in the leagues I played in and vocal in the stands. Whenever I stepped into the batter's box, I could hear her voice above the others as she urged me on with an emphatic "All right, let's go Brown!" Today was no different; I heard her loud and clear each time I stepped up to the plate.

Not that it helped all that much. You see, ever since I started my obsession with playing baseball, I was pretty much a "great glove, average stick" kind of player. I started on the street in front of our house, playing stickball against guys four and five years older and holding my own. That led to an obsession with "stoopball." Every day, weather permitting, I would take my glove and a pink rubber ball and play baseball by throwing that Spauldeen against the front steps of my house. Hour after hour, day after day, I pitched and caught that ball. I played complete games, doubleheaders, tripleheaders, always keeping track of the players and scores in my head.

Heck, I even announced the games out loud as I was playing them. I loved playing that game, and it remains my favorite from childhood. It definitely developed my fielding skills, but obviously did nothing for my hitting.

Though I played hundreds of real games and had a few seasons of moderate hitting success (I actually won the batting title and MVP award as a 15-year-old in Babe Ruth league), I had never, ever hit a home run. Never felt the elation of rounding the bases in a jog.

But that day, July 10, 1974, in front of the packed stadium, in the bottom of the sixth, I connected on a fastball thrown by The Park's ace, Matt McArrow. I'd like to tell you that I crushed the ball deep over the wall and onto the football field that was beyond the left center field fence, in front of the giant school building. But in reality, it was a high, lazy fly ball pulled sharply down the line. I was still running hard to second when I saw it land just beyond the fence, a foot or two inside the foul pole. I only got to jog to third base and home and heard my mom cheering the whole way. We won that game 6-5. I still have the ball. It's dirty and scuffed, but still has all of the inscriptions that I wrote on it that night at home. It's the only souvenir that I have from my days playing ball, which lasted through college and well into my thirties. And that remains the only home run I ever hit.

This coming Friday I've got the biggest game of my life and I haven't picked up a bat in over 15 years.

I need to hit one more home run.

Blog, Blog, Blog

We're pretty much in lockdown mode now. Just like a boxer or a team wraps themselves in a cocoon of privacy before the big match, we have retreated into the safety and comfort of our home and the company of our closest friends and family.

We've made so many calls and written so many emails that it seems like we're running a medical alert call center. The news about my upcoming surgery has spread like wildfire throughout the vast network of people who are following this like some serialized version of Brian's Song. I know that everyone wants to be kept updated, but honestly, I could use a publicist right about now.

I speak to Dr. Possibility up in Boston and tell him the surprising good news. When he hears that I am now operable, he is genuinely happy for us and says he agrees with the surgeon about possible follow-up treatment via the CyberKnife. We discuss post-surgical time frames and he sends a packet of gold-plated markers, little dowel-like objects that he says Dr. Hero should insert into the surgical field after he's finished so that the they can locate the exact spot, should we need to. He requests that the surgeons at Deaconess insert them for the same reasons and says that our doctor will clearly understand the need. We thank him and tell him how appreciative we are that he is in tune with linking the CyberKnife with traditional surgery.

I'm spending my days enjoying time with Linda and the kids, as we know that no matter the outcome, things are going to be mighty different with dad once the surgery is over. And there is that faintest of chances that this could be my final time with them. I'm not wasting any minutes. My brothers and I are on the phone several times a day. We haven't ever spoken this much, or with such passion, even when our folks were in their final days. They are optimistic and that comes through in every conversation. Gary has time available and is coming to the surgery, and Duane, who lives five hours away and can't take any more time off from work, is still trying to figure out a way to be here. I tell him he doesn't need to since I'm going to be out of it for some time and he can get the status directly from Gary or Linda. Laura is coming from Wyoming to be there for her sister and to be sure that they can get the real story on how it's going, then explain it in plain English.

During a quiet moment, Linda turns to me and says, "We really need to start a blog."

"A what?" I respond with that standard puzzled look on my face.

"A blog, to keep everyone updated during and after the surgery," she explains as I start to shake my head from side to side.

"Look, there are a ton of people who want to know what's happening, how it's going, how you're doing, and I'm not going to be in any shape or have the time to update all of them," she continued. "This way, we can post updates and they can follow along at their convenience."

"Honey, no one is going to want to follow my story, and I'm not sure it's fair for them to hear about the ups and downs of the fight," I counter. "I don't want to be responsible for depressing people on a regular basis."

Linda is getting exasperated with me as the conversation reaches its peak.

"First off, everyone we know wants to follow your story and they want to be frequently updated. Secondly, if it's too painful for them, then they don't have to read it."

I start to express my same concerns, but it's pretty obvious that I'm not going to be winning this battle.

"Okay, how do we do this?"

"There's a site called Carepages.com, let me show you how it works."

I set up my profile page, input the email addresses of the people we've been updating so far, and post my first entry:

Tuesday, 10/22/08

As I've said to many of you, the surgery is a go. It's going to be extensive and the recovery will be fairly long (10+ days in the hospital, another slow 4-6 weeks at home, and total recovery estimated to be 4+ months). They tell me to expect to lose 15-20% of my total body weight, which is 40+ lbs . . . hell of a way to diet!

Anyhow, spirits are good, looking forward to getting this tumor out of my body. Thanks for your prayers and positive thoughts.

Linda will take over the blog for the next few weeks. Talk to you all soon.

Livestrong. Be A Survivor.

Bob

I didn't invent that closing, but it sure seems appropriate.

And just like that, I'm a blogger.

I receive a boatload of responses wishing me well.

Twas the Night Before Surgery

The last few days have actually been pretty calm. A handful of calls from my closest of friends, but mostly it's been an eerily quiet time. Now, on the night before surgery, as I sit down at the dinner table, I'm filled with a building sense of hope. My brother, Gary, has come down from the Catskills, and Linda's sister, Laura, has flown in from Wyoming. Amanda will be here early tomorrow morning so she can take care of the kids while I'm in surgery. Despite my suggestion that it's really not necessary, it looks like my oldest brother, Duane, will be driving to New York from Cape Cod in the wee hours of the night so he can join the family for the long vigil during surgery.

This is going to be my last meal for quite some time and we've prepared one of my favorites: steak, salad, potatoes, and fresh, warm bread. There haven't been any restrictions on my diet and, in fact, the surgeon has encouraged me to keep my weight up, as that will serve me well during the inevitable post-surgery weight loss. No problem there, Doc. We open a couple of bottles of our favorite wine and make a toast for a successful surgery and a quick and complete recovery.

It's a great meal and I feel a surprising sense of peace and calm. I don't feel scared. I'm anxious of course, but not dreading it. It's been a whirlwind couple of weeks as the surgery has materialized, and I haven't really had the time to think through what's about to happen or to focus on the details of the process. My thoughts have been pigeonholed into the prospects for a cure.

Gary is incredibly optimistic. He just knows everything is going to be all right. And while it's clear that he blatantly ignores many of the grim details and statistics, I know that he truly believes it.

Linda continues to be confident as well. But she has had major surgery, back when her colon was resected, so she knows of the difficult days and weeks that lie ahead for me.

Laura, being a doctor, spends the evening answering my questions. She describes what the initial recovery might feel like in ICU, what kinds of assistance my body will require, and how my pain will be managed. She does a great job helping me understand and, frankly, it doesn't sound unbearable. But somehow, I think she's probably protecting me by giving me the bare minimum of information.

After all, this isn't her first rodeo. She knows what's really coming, and it isn't pretty.

Zero Hour

I'm sitting in a very comfortable recliner wrapped in a "Michelin Man" type paper robe. A separate motor is pumping slightly warmed air throughout the baffled chambers in the robe to keep me warm while I wait for the operating room to give the signal. We've all been awake since 4:00, and it's now about 7:30 in the morning. In the hour that we've been here, the attending nurse has prepped me with an IV, had me sign some final forms, and tried to keep us all informed. It's all incredibly routine, which is amazing, considering the monumental surgery that awaits me.

Before going to sleep last night, Linda and I spoke about the risks of the surgery and I told her my wishes for being kept alive, should something go terribly wrong during the operation and there was a life-or-death decision to be made. There are certain disabilities that I would be willing to survive, and there are some that, given the choice, I would not. I made sure that Linda understood my wishes.

Dr. Hero appears in the doorway, looking ready in his O.R. outfit, and he's accompanied by a tall man carrying a shoulder-held television camera. The cameraman is from the hospital and he'll be filming the operation for the hospital's use. The doctor asks if I'm ready and, after answering affirmatively, I ask him the same question. He smiles and says, "Then let's go."

I give Laura and Gary big hugs and thank them for being here with us. Duane is on his way from Massachusetts to be here for the surgery (and he plans to leave right afterwards). Linda and I hug for a while longer, whispering, "I love you."

Dr. Hero insists on us walking together to the O.R. and I must admit that it feels strangely empowering to not be lying on a gurney being wheeled around. Once we get to the O.R., things speed up considerably. I hop onto the operating table and begin to get the final prep by the nurses and anesthesiologist. After all the monitors and IVs are hooked up and ready to go, Dr. Hero comes to my side for a final chat.

"Any last questions?" he asks.

"How're you feeling, did you get enough sleep last night?" I joke.

He smiles broadly. "Well then, we'll get started."

"Okay, Doc, let's hit it out of the park."

Am I Alive?

"Mr. Brown, don't struggle. There is a ventilator in your throat helping you breathe. It's secured with tape, so you cannot remove it."

My eyes are closed, so I'm not seeing anything. The voice isn't at all familiar. I don't even understand what state of life I'm in. I do immediately realize one thing—there's a huge tube in my throat and it feels like I'm choking.

"Please don't fight it, let it do the breathing for you," the woman's voice reassures me.

But I am fighting it. Laura said that she highly doubted I would awaken with the ventilator. I was petrified of it. Now, as I start to wake up from the anesthesia, I'm incapable of moving, and I'm more uncomfortable than at any time since my diagnosis. I slowly open my eyes to see a nurse leaning over me. She informs me that I'm in recovery and that the tube will stay in until I'm breathing sufficiently on my own. I can't raise my arms, I can't raise my head. I don't feel any real pain, but I feel like I'm in a cocoon. I stare at the ceiling, try to avoid closing my throat around the tube, and give myself up to the machine.

In the next 30 minutes, I twice feel like the tube has become blocked. It feels exactly like when I was a kid swimming under water with a snorkel tube and my friend would clamp his palm down over the top, shutting off the air supply. That was a prank and it was sort of funny; this is definitely not. The nurse responds to my banging on the bed rail with my fist, rushing over to see what's wrong. Unfortunately, I cannot speak or communicate in any way. I'm not getting any air and there's no way to let her know! She realizes my predicament and shifts the tube slightly.

"Mr. Brown, there's nothing blocking the airway; you need to relax and stop fighting this. We'll remove the tube as soon as we can, about another 30 minutes."

I'm only a few minutes into my recovery, I'm beyond miserable, and I'm afraid that I won't survive it.

The recovery room nurses are true to their word, and just about 30 minutes later, they announce that they're going to remove the breathing tube. They tell me to let out a long sustained cough, and out it comes. Thank you.

Everything is instantly better. Not good, but better. Linda and Laura come to visit, leaning down to my ear, offering encouragement and love. I can only respond in a faint whisper. In addition to the now-removed ventilator down my throat, I have an IV in my right arm, a central PIC line exiting my neck, a gastric drainage tube coming out of the upper left side of my stomach, another gastric drainage tube for bile coming out of my right abdomen, and a catheter from my penis. Blood pressure cuffs, oxygen, and heart monitors—you name it, it's attached to me. I've got a giant, multi-layer bandage covering the 12-inch incision on my belly, and another smaller bandage over the opening in my neck where they removed the vein used to repair the damaged one in my pancreas. Like I said last night, Laura knew this was coming, and it isn't pretty.

But I'm still alive.

Most Whipple surgeries last about 6-7 hours. My surgery took 14.5 hours. Dr. Hero removed about half of my pancreas, my gall bladder, the upper portion of my duodenum, a small part of my stomach, and the main portion of my bile duct. He removed my damaged pancreatic vein and reconstructed the connection with one from my neck. An additional surgeon assisted with hundreds of micro-sutures within what was left of my pancreas, and I needed almost nine units of blood. My liver sustained significant damage.

But I'm still alive.

Dr. Hero comes to check on me and tells me that the surgery went well. I ask him in a whisper how I can ever express my thanks. He responds softly by asking me to keep his children in my prayers.

"I will, always."

My Kingdom for AriZona

As I progress through the first several days of recovery at a snail's pace, my initial impressions are simple. Firstly, whoever invented morphine and the self-administered pump, THANK YOU! Secondly, this catheter thing is not nearly as bad as feared. It's actually quite convenient, and really undetectable.

My pain is surprisingly tolerable because of the morphine, and other than the couple of times where I'm required to get up and walk (hunched over like Groucho Marx, but lacking any jump in my step), I spend all of my time lying in bed on my back.

I am not allowed anything to eat or drink, as my GI system needs time to heal. In fact, the path to my stomach is closed off and the drainage tube on my left side diverts anything that I swallow into a gallon-sized collection tub sitting on the floor. After a few days of using lip moisturizing wipes, I'm allowed the pleasure of ice chips and small sips of water. At the same time, I am parched beyond description. No matter how many sips of water I take, my lips and mouth are bone dry within seconds. It's making me very uncomfortable and miserable, but finally, after much pleading, one of my nurses agrees to let me have a sip of Linda's iced tea. I experience nirvana and immediately begin to conspire with her to bring me as much AriZona® Iced Tea as she can carry and conceal. She scours the bodegas of Washington Heights before arriving on her daily visits, we build our stash, hiding it on the floor behind my nightstand, and I "hit it" as often as possible. I consider writing a letter to the owners of the company to tell them what their product means to me, but decide to leave them a portion of my estate instead.

It doesn't take much for the nurses to be on to me.

"Mr. Brown, what is going on here?" my day nurse inquires in a rather loud and perturbed voice after seeing my drainage bag filled to capacity.

She just began her shift and I had been gulping the AriZona all night. The assistant also enters the room and they advise me that I'm supposed to be drinking little sips of water to alleviate the dryness, not drinking entire bottles of banned liquids.

"First of all, that bag should be filling up once every couple of days, not every couple of hours! And secondly, you need to get ready for your leakage test," she admonishes.

"What test?"

"We need to see how your connections are healing. Before we allow you any food or liquids, we need to clamp off the drainage tube and you won't be allowed anything by mouth for six hours."

Before I can even start to envision the agony of six hours without any liquids, she adds, "Then we'll unclamp you, see if there are any leaks, and if all is okay, we'll clamp you off again and you'll go 24 more hours without any liquids."

I can't even comprehend going through those test periods without liquids, since I can't make it more than a couple of minutes now. I elect to ignore that and fight back in the present.

"What's the difference? The liquid is going right out for now, it's giving me real relief and pleasure, and when I'm ready for the test, then I'll deal with it."

The nurse says she'll check with my doctor and I agree that I'll follow his rules.

He tells the nurses to let me drink whatever I want, but be prepared for when I'm ready for the test. Chalk one up for the patient.

We should have bought stock in AriZona Iced Tea.

Too Good to be True

The next couple of days continue to go well, with more and more tubes being removed. I'm down to one IV and two drainage tubes. Despite my demands for general anesthesia, they remove the catheter with very little discomfort. I begin to pee standing up next to the bed, using a hand-held urinal. It's quite a challenge, as I have to hold the urinal with one hand and hold my privates with my other hand. Unfortunately, that doesn't leave me with any hands to hold myself up. During one of the first times I'm doing this, my privacy curtain falls down. Not just the curtain, but the entire track, rod, and curtain, all at once. That leaves me standing there completely exposed to my roommate's very surprised wife and family.

"Sorry, nice to meet you," I say while turning away, now exposing my completely bare backside. This is much better.

My roommate's wife shifts her chair, but there's no real avoiding the poor guy standing there in front of her.

The maintenance crew is there in a jiffy. Unfortunately, they can't repair the track since it's woefully outdated, and I spend the rest of my stay in open view of any other occupants of the room. It's a good thing I've never been bashful.

The very next day the doctors inform me that we're going ahead with the clamp test. (No wonder the doctor allowed me to drink at will. He knew it would be short-lived.). It will last for 6 hours at first, then if all goes well, 24 hours.

I take a good long drink of tea, then the doctors clamp off the stomach drainage tube. This means that any liquids in my mouth (basically, normal saliva, etc.) will make their way down to my stomach instead of out the drainage tube. This way, they can determine if the connections have healed and I'm ready to start consuming liquids.

Within a minute or two, I'm thirsty, but surprisingly, I seem to be handling the discomfort much better. I'm sure it's the knowledge that I can't drink that helps me get through it. I try to watch TV (I'm particularly fond of the Food Channel, which if you think about it, is pretty self-torturous), then get some sleep. Before you know it, the time has passed and they're back in checking on the results.

I pass, which means that very little fluid leaked, and now we can proceed to the 24-hour clamp off. But first, I get 15 minutes to "refresh" myself. The nurses once again instruct me to drink very little, but are kind enough to bring me two large cups of water. I pass those up for a quick quart of iced tea. Ahhh.

As you can imagine, the 24 hours are significantly more difficult to endure. I almost put myself into a trance-like state, trying hard not to over-stimulate myself. It works and somehow I do make it through the test. And I pass! The tube will be capped and I'll be on to liquids pronto.

Shortly after that good news, the cleaning lady knocks on my door and asks if she can come in to straighten up the room. She's a slightly older woman, probably in her mid-sixties, slim, friendly, and, despite being African American, reminds me of my Nana, my mom's mom.

Every morning since I've been in the regular room, she comes in to clean up, and while she's doing it, she's usually singing. For the last few days we've been singing together and it has really been fun, as she's lifted my spirits despite my physical discomfort. Today is no different and we're belting out that classic Frankie Valli song,

"You're just too good to be true,
Can't take my eyes off of you,
You'd be like heaven to touch,
I want to hold you so much . . ."

"At long last love has arrived,
And I thank God I'm alive,
You're just too good to be true,
Can't take my eyes off of you."

Just then, Dr. Hero's team enters the room to do my morning checkup and they stop and stare in disbelief at the carryings on that are happening in the room. We continue with the song leading up to the big finish, when the doctor himself enters the room, parting his team right down the middle as he walks in. He takes a good, long look at us, then at his team, then back at us. A big smile breaks out across his face as he joins us in singing,

"Oh, pretty baby, don't bring me down, I pray.
Oh, pretty baby, now that I found you, stay
And let me love you, baby.
Let me love you."

Pretty cool doctor. Like I said before, he's an honest-to-goodness hero.

But then, just when everything is going so well and my discharge looks only days away, I wake up later that night with a high fever and my incision oozing like crazy. I'm burning up and I'm soaking through my bandages faster than they can be changed.

By morning it's clear that I have developed some sort of infection. I immediately undergo a CT scan and an ultrasound to determine what's happening inside my belly.

The tests reveal nothing unusual, other than a general infection, which they begin treating with IV antibiotics. Once again, I'm off of any liquids via mouth. And so, just like that, I've suffered my first setback. Only time will tell how this plays out, but it's now certain that I won't be sent home in the next few days.

Maybe it was too good to be true.

Almost Home

The next few days are uncomfortable as I struggle to get rid of this infection. I'm off the morphine pump now, getting my pain relief via IV injections of Dilaudid. It, too, is an amazing pain reliever and it makes the setback tolerable.

The nurses and aides are incredibly compassionate and are always available at the push of the call button. There's also an intern working the floor who helps change the dressing on my wound more times than I can remember, always with meticulous care.

The physical therapist is a small guy who's a cross between Billy Crystal and Richard Simmons. His job is to get me competent at getting in and out of bed or a chair. He soon has me walking up and down the hallways using a walker, then progressing to a claw-footed cane. It feels like the bottom of my abdomen is going to fall to the floor as I slowly pass the nurses' stations and other patient rooms. He continually peppers me with encouragement interspersed with corny one-liners. I tell him that he needs to be on Dilaudid. But son of a gun, he does get me moving.

Linda visits me every day. It's a long drive from our home in central Jersey and sometimes I implore her to come as early as possible so she can bring some liquid contraband. That means fighting the rush hour commuter traffic and consequently being a bit tired and cranky when she arrives. But she's always there, supporting me every step of the way.

She continues to post updates to my medical blog every day, letting everyone in on the ups, downs, and some of the silliness that's happening. One of our favorite things to do is read the numerous messages that are being posted back to the blog. They constantly bring smiles to our faces and tears to my eyes.

After our post about scouring the neighborhood for AriZona Iced Tea:

"Count on the Browns to always find the humor and silver lining . . . can't wait to see the AZ commercial during the Super Bowl this year."

"Since my 401k is in the dumper, I plan on buying stock in Arizona iced tea tomorrow. Keep on drinking."

"I never thought that reading a care page site could be so funny. Your updates are more fun to read than the newspaper comics. Never would have guessed it, but it's awesome!"

Then one from a co-worker of Linda's, whom I've never met:

"My name is Jim, and I've been following your story from the sidelines. What a battle you've been through. What a tremendous support network you have—a real cast of characters. There's a lot of love being shared and a lot of prayers being spoken. There's even been a lot of fun in the midst of all this. It's inspiring to everyone at all levels."

Many of the messages talk about how inspiring my journey and my positive attitude are. That's totally wrong. They're the ones who are inspiring me!

This blog thing is pretty cool. In my increasingly isolated world, it keeps me connected to my network of supporters. I can't believe I'm wrong again.

An Advocate is Born

My third roommate arrived today. He was just diagnosed with PC and is scheduled for a Whipple surgery in the coming days. He's uncomfortable and still in the early haze of confusion that surrounds newly diagnosed patients.

As I listen to the conversations that are taking place behind his privacy curtain between him and his family and doctors, it brings back memories of the many we had, except we had months to think it through and they're trying to process everything within a day or two.

After another round of updates, his doctors leave and it's clear to me that I have assets he can use—experience and knowledge. I gingerly ease myself out of bed and unplug my IV pole from the wall. It beeps twice to confirm that it's on battery power. I shuffle to the end of my bed and swing around to the other side of his curtain where I encounter my roommate and his wife and brother. She's already met my backside on a few occasions.

"Hi, I'm Bob, and I'm sorry, but I couldn't help but overhear your conversations. I'm sorry to hear about your diagnosis," I say, leaning about 80 degrees as I hold the IV pole in one hand and the claw-foot cane in the other. Not exactly your picture of post-surgical health.

"Hi Bob, I'm Sonny. I've got a malignant pancreatic tumor and I'm scheduled to have something called a Whipple at the end of this week; it doesn't sound good at all."

"Well, Sonny, it's nice to meet you. You are a very lucky man!"

He and his family stare back at me with a quizzical look tinged with sympathy for someone who's clearly on drugs and delusional. I recount the long and winding road to my own Whipple, then expand upon much of what his doctors have already said, but in layman's terms. He and his wife ask a ton of questions, from how it all started, to how I'm feeling right now, and everything in between.

They listen intently as I relate my story. It's obvious that the information I'm giving them is important and very much appreciated, but there's something more. It's the fact that I'm a fellow PC patient, that I've been through exactly what they'll be experiencing soon, and that I'm alive and standing there in front of them. It shows them that it's doable. It proves that people with PC can not only get to the tunnel, but can come out the other side. It feels good to be able to give back and to be able to help with something I now know very well.

Without deliberately trying, it's clear that I'm giving them inspiration and hope in their battle.

Mine too.

Homecoming!

Well, it's been 17 days since my surgery, I've been on solid food for the past 3 days, and they removed my IV yesterday. I'm on oral antibiotics and I seem to be able to perform my basic bodily functions pretty much unassisted. I must admit, however, that walking to the bathroom 10 feet away, using the real commode, and returning to the bed is an agonizing and moderately painful 20 minute ordeal. To my doctors, all of this qualifies me to go home.

One of the residents who has been keeping an eye on me comes in to announce that before I go home, they'll need to remove my gastric drain tube. That's done while I'm awake, no anesthetic. They simply tell you to breathe normally (are you kidding?) and they pull it out. Right through my abdominal wall! It's the very definition of the "heebie-jeebies."

The rest of the day I slowly get my things in order and get my discharge marching orders. I'm excited to go home, but really apprehensive about being able to function well enough not to be a burden to Linda and her mom (yup, Helen's back at our house to help with my recovery).

Before we leave, we meet with Dr. Hero to go over my pathology reports from the surgery. By now, we've surmised that the news cannot be all that great, or he would have given it to us sooner. It appears that he wanted to let me heal as much as possible before having the conversation. Unfortunately, we're right.

"We hit a triple, not the home run," he says with a surprisingly upbeat tone.

"I was able to remove the entire physical tumor, but we didn't get totally clean margins, particularly around the area where the tumor infiltrated your vein. You've got some cleanup work to do, so I recommend that you seek out the CyberKnife treatment and set up an appointment with my oncology colleague."

Linda and I take the news in stride. Like I said, it's not a total surprise. What's really surprising is that I leave the hospital that day believing that I can get this "cleanup" work done, move forward, and survive.

Dr. Hero seems confident that we've had an overall good outcome, and his confidence obstructs my understanding of what's really happened. You see, what I'm failing to accept now is what I knew like the back of my hand before the surgery: The Whipple surgery is "all-in." You either exit with clean margins—a victory (the home run)—or you don't, and you lose. Everything I read explained it that way. It was very black and white. If they get all of the cancer out, you've got a chance for a complete cure. If they don't, then your chance for the cure is gone.

As Linda drives us home, taking extreme care to drive lightly over the many cracks and crevices in the road that shoot daggers through my belly, it's pretty clear that I've lost, but somehow, we don't believe that.

A Week at a Time

In many regards, it's great to be back at home. I get to see my kids and sleep in my own bed. I have my choice of food and drinks (no, I'm no longer craving iced tea; now it's tall glasses of cold milk), and I certainly have a lot more channel choices on the TV.

The flip side is that I'm not capable of doing very much. Getting up from bed or a chair is difficult and moderately painful. It's the same for sitting down. I'm still popping Percocets like Tic Tacs®, and while they're keeping the pain tolerable, they leave me pretty groggy much of the time. Bathroom activities continue to take forever, and I spend most of my time resting in bed or on the couch, or sleeping.

The kids are great, but they can't get too close to me, since my wound still has a ways to go to heal. We hug lightly and talk, but they give me a lot of space. It's going to be a while before I can pick them up again.

Eating is a major challenge. It's difficult to keep myself sitting upright at the table, and I can't eat more than a few tablespoons at a time. My stomach has not only shrunk, but is still traumatized, so it's slow-going to get food into my body. And while it's good to be in my own bed, I could still use the power lift features of those hospital beds.

A nurse is coming to the house several times a week to check my vitals, inspect and change the dressing on my incision site, and generally ensure that I'm making consistent progress. The rest of the time, it's up to Linda, and she's been changing my dressing like a professional.

The doctors have told me not to expect to feel anywhere near normal until a minimum of three months after surgery, so I'm trying to be realistic in my own expectations.

After I've got one week at home under my belt, I hobble over to my computer and begin my first blog posting since just prior to the surgery. It's short and sweet, with just the basics of how I'm doing. I convey that I don't have the energy to do much, and apologize for not personally posting sooner. I thank everyone from the bottom of my heart for their outpouring of good wishes and encouragement and sign off by telling them that my spirits are high.

I receive tons of responses, mostly saying how great it is to hear from me, stressing patience, and encouraging me to do everything from eating more to eating less, from resting as much as possible to getting out soon to play a round of golf. One of the crazier posts insists that I need to take the 'Vette out for a spirited ride at 90 or 100 mph. All of them offer prayers, love, and support, and many mimic my own closing by telling me to "Stay strong, be a survivor." My favorite comes from a former assistant who ends her message with "You are my hero."

It seems that the energy and inspiration connected with the blog are flowing equally in both directions.

Faith and the Holidays

It's holiday season, and that usually means lots of activities, shopping, anticipation, excitement, and eating. Lots and lots of eating. Since I'm the one who normally does the cooking, it's nice to have Helen here to help us prepare for the big Thanksgiving feast. Of course, I'll only be able to eat a few bites, but the smell of turkey, stuffing, and homemade pies filling the house that morning is tremendously comforting.

By mid-morning, the kids join me in my familiar and necessary place on the family room couch to watch the Macy's parade. I'd been to the parade a few times. When I was a child I went with my godmother, and when Linda and I met, we made it an annual ritual to go to NYC and stay in a midtown hotel close to the parade route. Each time we'd head uptown to 81st Street and Columbus Avenue the night before to watch the big balloons being inflated around the corner from my father's liquor store. Since I was always helping out at the store during the holidays, I spent many a night before Thanksgiving watching those giant helium-filled icons come to life. In recent years, the inflating of the balloons became a much more commercial event, with crowd control barriers and food and souvenir vendors everywhere. Nonetheless, the whole event was unique and fun to experience. The parade the next day is the granddaddy of parades, and has to be seen in person to be believed.

That day will have to wait for Taylor and Colton, as their dad is fortunate just to be able to sit upright and watch it on TV today. We gather and watch, with a small fire crackling in the fireplace. They love the colors, singing, and dancing, but like most kids, they love the big balloons. They ask when we can go see the parade. I tell them it'll be real soon. Just as soon as Dad gets better. My favorite part is the end, when Santa comes riding in on his grand sleigh. The kids love it too. Christmas (and Christmas presents) is just around the corner!

After the parade, the movie *Miracle on 34th Street* comes on. It's become a tradition for TV to show it right after the parade, and it's another great way to put you in that holiday spirit. It's my all-time favorite holiday movie, and even though the kids quickly lose interest, I watch it with a comforting joy. There are many parts of the movie that I adore, but this time watching it, I notice that there's a particular scene that seems written just for me. When lawyer Fred Gailey is justifying his defense of Kris Kringle, he tells Doris, "Faith is believing when common sense tells you not to." I start to tear up immediately. He just described my whole state of mind.

Thanksgiving ends with a few morsels of apple pie, and soon after, Helen is on her way back home to Colorado. The rest of the holiday season comes quickly. I'm getting around a whole lot better, and I'm contributing to the household more and more each day. One of the more interesting reactions is that I seem to be crying. A lot! Not a day goes by where I don't burst into tears at least once. Sometimes it's when the kids try to cheer me up by acting ever so silly. And other times it comes over me while I'm watching some sentimental movie that seems to be on TV every other minute during the holidays. But what's crazy is that it's happening even when I'm watching things like the Hallmark Christmas card commercials. And of course it's happening whenever Taylor or Colton comes up and gives me a giant hug, or they tell me they love me.

When I mention this to the doctors, they say I'm suffering from a type of post-traumatic stress syndrome, and that it's not unusual at all.

Just a few more battle scars from the cancer war.

As the New Year dawns, my strength and overall functioning are much improved. They're nowhere near what they were prior to the surgery, but the surgeon has removed the staples and drainage tube, the wound is pretty much healed, and my mobility is a lot better. I get the okay to start driving again, and Dr. Hero and I discuss the next steps in the battle plan.

"Go see the CyberKnife team up in Boston and make an appointment with Dr. Shoulda, an oncologist here at NYP. It's time to start the next phase of your treatments," he says with his usual calm and optimistic demeanor.

I make the appointments for the coming weeks, and at the direction of Dr. P at Deaconess, I get a new CT scan of the surgical field in my abdomen. He'll need that to pinpoint the CyberKnife treatments. This is all good, things are moving ahead, and I'm feeling excited about "cleaning up" what's left of this nasty cancer inside of me.

I continue to blindly ignore the fact that the surgery was not a total success.

One night, Linda and I sit down and watch the Barbara Walters special starring Patrick Swayze and his wife, Lisa. Dr. Hero is in the program, having been interviewed right around the time of my surgery. The show is informative and inspiring, as Patrick is clearly fighting this as hard as he can. He's been shooting a new television series during his chemo treatments, and while he still possesses that Swayze charm, it's obvious that the disease is taking a terrible toll on him.

Ms. Walters' questions about his prognosis are particularly difficult to watch. His and Lisa's answers are similar to what Linda and I have had to talk about. The interview ends on a very sad note for me, when Barbara asks him how long he thinks he will live and what he hopes for in the future.

"Hell, I'd say five years is pretty wishful thinking. Two years is likely if you're gonna believe statistics. I want to last until they find a cure. I'll keep fighting until the fight doesn't match up to the quality of life."

I'm coming up on the one year anniversary of my diagnosis.

Could it really be one down, one to go?

The Last Big Drop

Right near the end of the ride on the Cyclone, there are a couple of wicked dips and turns. Because of the timing, they rock you around more than you'd expect, because you think the ride is over.

The appointment with our new oncologist is scheduled for 3:00 p.m. At 5:30, Linda and I are still waiting to be called in to see him. We've seen about a dozen people come and go, some arriving after us, yet they see him before us. We've been to a lot of doctors in the past year, and spent a ton of time waiting in the appropriately-named outer rooms, but nothing compares to this. *He must be some doctor*, I think. I hope. Several of the waiting patients open up to us.

"He's amazing, I've been on his new GTX chemo program for several months now, and my tumors are dramatically shrinking!" says one woman in her early forties, who's there with her doting husband.

"But he does run a bit behind schedule," she adds with a warm smile.

At 6:00 p.m., when we are the last two people left in the waiting room, we are called into his consult room. He enters with a plain manila folder with my name written on the tab. As he sits down opposite us, he opens the folder to reveal a single piece of paper, which he seems to be reviewing for the first time.

"Why are you here?" he asks.

"Our surgeon, Dr. Hero, has given me the green light for the next phase of my treatment program, and he suggested that I come to see you," I respond, surprised that he doesn't already know that.

He looks at both of us, then down to the paper, and back up at us.

"You have a lot of tumor left inside of you, and I don't think I can help you at this point. You needed to come see me six months ago, before you were treated elsewhere," he states with a crushing arrogance.

Dr. Shoulda then really gets going, claiming that I've made a big mistake in my initial choice of treatment center. If I had come to him first, I could have been put on the GTX program. It has shown a promising record of changing inoperable patients to Whipple-ready status, and most impressively, two-thirds of those patients exit the surgery with negative margins.

"Your margins are positive, there's a lot of cancer left in your body, particularly in the area where the tumor invaded your vein," he continues with a callousness that starts to rile both of us.

The tirade continues as he trashes the hospital that we chose, and he finishes with an ominous prediction.

"In cases like this, the cancer comes back. It always comes back."

Once again, we're blindsided. We didn't see this coming, and Linda and I are more than taken aback, we're pissed! Genius doctor or not, Linda is ready to jump the desk and let this son of a bitch have a few blows to his giant-ego-sized head. We take a deep breath, hold off on the planned assault, and ask him his bottom line.

"Honestly, I don't treat patients like you. I'd have to think about a plan. But here are two ideas. First, I'll prescribe a drug named Tarceva for you to take daily in pill form. It's been used to treat lung cancer, and has recently been extended to the treatment of PC. It's worth a shot. Secondly, why don't you call a colleague of mine at Sloan Kettering here in the city? Let's see if she views your case the same way."

We take the prescription, the doctor reference, get up, and leave. We don't shake his hand.

On the ride down to the lobby in the empty elevator, our blood is boiling.

"What an asshole. Genius or not, nobody has the right to speak to a patient that way," Linda vents.

I agree, and by the time we're in our car and heading back over the GW Bridge, my anger gives way to the reality of what our long day has confirmed. The surgery was only partially successful, and in the war on pancreatic cancer, partial success is really a total loss.

After another long, sleepless night, I get right to it in the morning. It's amazing how my mind is able to deflect the negatives and re-focus on the few remaining options. I call Sloan Kettering and explain to the nurse how I've been referred to the doctor, along with a brief outline of my case. The nurse is short with me and says matter-of-factly that I should gather all of my records and forward them to the office. They will review the file and if they want to see me, they will call me back to set up an appointment. The process should take at least five to six weeks.

"The Sloan Kettering option is out," I tell Linda with my hopes fading faster than tears on my sleeve.

I grab my car keys and head to the imaging center to retrieve the report on my recent scans. When I pull into the parking lot, I'm still coming to grips with the fact that the CyberKnife treatment now appears to be my last option. I'm anxious, which is normal, but not overly concerned, as getting results has become a fairly routine task in a journey filled with events that have been anything but. The receptionist prints out the report, seals it in a clean white envelope, and cheerfully hands it to me, wishing me a nice day.

Inside my car in the parking lot, I open the envelope and peruse the contents. The first report is about the upper chest and lung area, and the summary states that there's nothing remarkable to report. Good news, as expected. On to page two.

CT Results—Abdomen
Summary: Multiple lesions noted on liver, consistent with metastatic disease.

My brain doesn't comprehend what my eyes have just read. I read that one sentence over and over again. I never get to the rest of the report. After a few moments, it becomes crystal clear. It's moved to my liver. I have stage 4 pancreatic cancer.

End of the ride, thanks for coming.

Once again, I'm alone when I read this devastating news, and I slowly drive the 15 minute trip back to my house in a complete state of panic. It's as if a dense fog has descended upon me inside of my car. I can only see a short distance directly in front of me. I'm not aware of anything happening around the sides or back of the car. I'm not even sure how I'm operating the controls. My head is exploding with the harsh reality of what has happened. Surviving this has always been a dream that came with longest of odds. Now that dream is over. Now we've moved into miracle territory.

I'm still in a paralyzing haze when I stumble into our house and head straight for the office where Linda is working.

"Oh, hi. I just finished posting an update to the Carepages, telling everyone about our visit with Dr. S yesterday," she says rather proudly as she looks up from the keyboard.

"It's in my liver," I whisper as I hand her the report.

She takes the news calmly, but it's clear that the bombshell I've just delivered is of the nuclear kind. She posts a second update that very minute.

CAT Scan Results—January 7, 2009

No sooner did I hit the send button, Bob walked in the door with the test results. There is no easy way to say this . . . he now has multiple lesions on his liver, so the cancer has metastasized. He will not qualify for CyberKnife.

We are in shock and will let you know when we know more, but felt it was important to let you all know.

The number of responses are overwhelming. So many write of miracles and biblical passages. Everyone implores me to not give up. Everyone who's been following this journey has just been deeply hurt.

In the almost 12 months that we've been on this journey, there have been many twists and turns. There have been many ups and downs. This is rock bottom. Taylor is home from school, and she and Colton are playing in the family room with Amanda. I walk up to them like a zombie, kneel down, and squeeze them as tightly as I can. I don't want to ever let go.

Later that night I speak with Dr. Laura to discuss the one-two punch I've just been given. I tell her that I'm going to call Cancer Treatment Centers of America. I have nowhere else to turn, and I need what they offer—hope. She agrees completely. She also knows that everything she feared is materializing. All of the treatment options have evaporated, and the optimism has devolved into the awful confirmation of the end game of this disease. She's so upset that at the end of our call, she breaks down while telling me that it's time to start writing to my children in a daily journal.

The Tiniest Sliver

I stay awake almost the entire night. Unfortunately, I don't see any commercials for CTCA. When the morning arrives, I slowly get out of bed and get Taylor ready for school. It's the small things that get you through.

In this battle for my life, I've had a ton of people refer to me as their "hero." They're inspired by my "heroic" battle against the toughest of odds. I've always felt uncomfortable with those characterizations. I wish I could say that there was a big "John Wayne" moment where I rose up to fight the cancer. But in reality, all I've been doing is getting out of bed every day and facing the battle head on. Maybe that's what a hero really does.

I help Taylor get dressed, make her cinnamon toast for breakfast, walk her to the school bus, and give her a big hug and a kiss goodbye. Just doing normal stuff on a terrible day. Maybe that's what a hero does.

Maybe I really am a hero.

Just after Taylor leaves, my friend Jeff calls and tells me that he's in my area and would like to stop by. Jeff used to work for me and we stayed close after we moved on to different companies. We were always conjuring up businesses and plans that we could put into practice. Unfortunately, we never moved forward on any, and ended up in different industries. So while we spoke often, we hardly saw each other at all.

Five minutes later, he's ringing my doorbell. I tell him how much I appreciate him being there and we hug tightly as he comes into the foyer. We spend the next half hour just talking. He's a man with a lot of faith in his life, and when I tell him that it looks like it'll take a real miracle to save me now, he puts his arm around my shoulders and tells me, "Bob, they happen all the time. It will happen for you."

Later that morning, Dr. Hero calls me. He has just finished reviewing the CT scan and report.

"Bob, I'm not so sure that what they're reporting on these scans is metastatic disease. I was inside of you; I inspected your liver before the surgery began. It was clean. If you had lesions, I would have called off the surgery. I believe it's possible that what the scans are showing now is liver necrosis, dead areas that were damaged during the surgery. Remember that I had to shut off the blood supply to your liver for a period of time during the surgery. What I'm seeing on your scans is similar to what I've seen in other patients of mine who were at similar points in their recovery. Don't panic just yet."

Once again, my most trusted doctor comes through. During the darkest of days, he provides a small sliver of light. Maybe *that's* what a hero really does.

The Final Option

Maybe it was Dr. Hero's phone call, or maybe it was the complete exhaustion, but with the assistance of Xanax and Ambien, I finally get some sleep that night. The next morning I start on two important tasks.

First I start to work on a letter to Linda, accompanied by a worksheet containing all of the financial ins and outs of the family Brown. Since I've been the one managing the finances, investments, assets, etc., it's critical that she has a single place to go to see everything. I list all of our accounts with addresses, telephone numbers, and account numbers. I also give her suggestions as to what to do with things like my life insurance proceeds (pay off the house and invest the rest in the kids' college funds) and my cars (get my brother Gary to sell them). It's so sad, yet kind of empowering to write down this information. I realize that the prospect of my death is getting more and more certain as my options have evaporated, but I feel surprisingly strong again as I get to direct some aspect of my family's future. For the first time in a long while, I feel like I'm contributing again. I guess it might be the last time.

I'm not ready to begin writing to my children. That thought brings more pain than I can bear right now, and honestly, I have no idea what to say. I do come up with an interesting thought: Perhaps I will get birthday cards for each of them for the next 10-or-so years. I could write a short "letter" in each of them, maybe include a gift, maybe a favorite picture of us together when they were small and I was healthy. I stop and wonder if that will bring smiles to their faces or tears to their eyes. This is just the worst.

When they come downstairs for breakfast that morning I tell them how much I love them, then point to their hearts and tell them, "No matter what happens to me, or wherever I am, all you have to do is put your hand on your heart, and that's where I'll be."

Next, I make an important call. Living in a large metropolitan area with a number of prestigious, internationally known medical centers, it seems rather silly to be placing a call to a cancer hospital that I see advertised on television. I don't know of anyone who has been to Cancer Treatment Centers of America (CTCA), and I haven't been referred to any doctor there. All I know is that I need what they're advertising—compassion, hope, and the willingness to fight. I pick up the telephone and dial the 800 number. The call is answered by an oncology information specialist named Manny Brown. Good name.

From the very first moment, everything about this place seems completely different from anyplace else we've been. Linda and I are treated with incredible courtesy and helpfulness. After I give him a brief history of my case, I cut to where I am now.

"Manny, my latest scans show that the cancer has metastasized to my liver," I explain, holding my emotions together.

"Bob, we see a lot of patients at this stage of the disease; in fact, many see us as you do, the last resort. Our doctors are well-versed in pancreatic cancer and we're producing some great outcomes. I'm sure you've heard of Peggy and Roger," he declares with a low-key sense of pride.

I confirm that I have read about the hospital's stage 4 star patients on their website. It's strange because it feels like I'm hearing the commercial again, but at the same time, it's a breath of fresh air to hear someone speak so positively about this disease.

Manny then takes over the conversation completely.

"Okay, Bob and Linda, this is how we work. You don't have to do anything more than show up here. We will retrieve your medical records from your doctors. We will speak to your insurance carrier to get the necessary approvals. We will make your travel arrangements to get here. As a patient, Bob, you'll travel free. Linda will also travel free for this first visit. We want you to come to the center in Zion, Illinois, as we're more experienced in pancreatic cancer there. Your first visit for evaluation will be from three to five days. We will pick you up at the airport and bring you to your hotel. That is free of charge also. The hotel offers a special rate of $40.00 a night to CTCA patients. A free shuttle will bring you to and from the hospital and it runs all day. You and Linda are welcome to eat all of your meals in the cafeteria free of charge."

On and on he goes, as Linda and I struggle to believe what we're hearing. It sounds too good to be true. And it sounds crazy. How can they offer this?

"Let me see," he continues, "and we can see you this coming Tuesday."

I give him all of the information about my medical insurance and my doctors, and he informs us that he will confirm everything back to us in less than 24 hours. We hang up the telephone, seeing that the LED timer clocked the call at over an hour.

"We've never experienced anything like that," I say to Linda with true amazement.

"Looks like we've got another option," she says as she kisses my cheek.

A Couple of Entries from the Blog

Baby, it's cold outside—Jan 21, 2009

Hey Everyone,

Linda and I are in Zion, Illinois, at CTCA, at the Wisconsin border, and it is really cold here.

So far, CTCA is as advertised. The staff and doctors are incredibly caring and friendly. The initial processes have been very well done, and the scheduled appointments are kept right on time (certainly different from other places).

We met with a new oncologist. His name is Dr. Red Sox, and other than the fact that he is young, and worse, a fan of the Boston baseball team, we came away feeling confident in him and his knowledge of my situation. He had already read my entire file before we met with him, and after going through my last year with me, seemed fully up to speed on my case.

Dr. Red Sox believes that Dr. Hero's theory may be correct. He saw that the report from the surgery refers to the artery feeding the right side of the liver as being cut off for a period of time. The new lesions on my liver are all on the right side. It's not unusual to have lesions on the liver. It is very unusual for them to be all on one side. Indeed, it could be dead areas, not tumors. We need to find out. He has ordered a complete set of new tests which I'll have completed by tomorrow. Unfortunately, all of the scans and tests have limitations due to the point in time where I am in my recovery from the surgery. They'll compare them to the previous scans and see if they can reach a conclusion on my liver. We could also proceed to biopsies. Anyway, this will be an important step in determining the next course of treatment. The roller coaster continues . . .

But . . . a ray of hope. Stay tuned.

Livestrong. Be A Survivor.

Bob

Then, a few days later . . .

Well, well, well . . . you just never know!—Jan 23, 2009

Hey everyone,

A funny thing happened on the way to stage 4 cancer . . . it appears that it hasn't happened. After reviewing all of the new tests and comparing them with the previous tests from just a month ago, as well as back in the summer . . . then comparing to my surgical report . . . the doctors here agree with my surgeon, and believe that it is very unlikely that the cancer has spread to my liver. They believe that biopsies are unnecessary at this time.

The lesions that are there have already started to reduce in size (which is the sign of dead areas regenerating), and the PET scan shows no new areas for significant concern. On the other hand, with this disease there is always reason for concern. While I'm not out of the woods, this is clearly the best possible news that could have occurred. We come back in 6 weeks for follow-up testing, then we're hopefully back on track to use CyberKnife or some other super-duper radiation therapy to attack the remaining microscopic cancer cells around what's left of my pancreas (cells which did not light up on the PET scan I might add).

Linda and I are officially discharged and we're heading back to balmy NJ tonight (Zion, Ill. will be near zero this weekend).

It's nice to be able to deliver some good news. Thanks for your thoughts and prayers.

Livestrong. Be A Survivor.

Bob

We receive so many messages back, all saying pretty much the same thing as this one:

"Brownie, you and Linda are the poster children for hope! God bless you both, keep up the fight! This 'thing' WILL NOT WIN!!!"

What an incredible few weeks. Even when you feel as if you've experienced everything related to this journey, there are a few surprises left. I don't know if we've snatched victory from the jaws of defeat, but I do know one thing for certain—we're still in the game!

The Smell of Freshly Cut Grass

As the weeks go by, I am definitely feeling better. My weight has stabilized at about 190, down more than 40 pounds from before surgery, and my appetite seems to be very good. I've even begun to have the occasional glass of wine with dinner again. I'm now essentially off of painkillers, and the random physical discomfort is pretty tolerable. My strength has improved to where I'm now able to lift Taylor and Colton to give them hugs (no, not at the same time!). I'm taking upwards of 25 pills a day, including prescriptions, supplements, and the Tarceva.

I haven't begun to create any kind of bucket list, but after seeing the movie, I intend on doing things now that I may have put off before. First up is going to Tampa, Florida, to spend time in the warm weather and see the Yanks in action during spring training.

There's something special about the start of a new baseball season. The winter has ended, it's beginning to get warm, and there's a sense of hope and optimism that surrounds the beginning of spring training. It's been close to 20 years since I was in Florida to see the pre-season, and this time, it's that hope and optimism that bring me here.

Standing for the national anthem, I look out over field covered in lush green grass, my favorite players standing at attention waiting for the 13-year-old vocalist to begin. I took this trip alone, as I wanted this experience to be personal and private, yet I now find myself standing between two strangers who are staring at me as tears stream from beneath my sunglasses and my shoulders heave up and down from my quiet sobs of joy.

Being at this game is monumental to me. There have been a thousand times where I've thought that I would never live to see another ball game, and yet, here I stand—proud, humbled, and grateful.

"Sorry, I'm just really thrilled to be here to watch these guys play," I say to my new companions after the song ends.

"Yeah, I understand," says the older guy with the silver hair and beat up Yankees hat. "Here, have some peanuts, go Yanks."

Just a normal day at the ballpark.

Let the Battle Continue

"Jeter looked in great shape; I think he's going to have a big year. And A-Rod, you should have seen the homer he hit; it must have gone 50 feet past the center field wall!" I tell Dr. Red Sox as he sits down to give me the results of my recent scans.

Linda and I are back at CTCA. The place continues to amaze us. Everywhere we go, we run into other cancer patients, and it's that interaction that helps make this place so different. We get to hear stories of courage and success. We meet other PC patients who are quick to relate their own battles. There's a genuine camaraderie amongst the patients and their caregivers that breeds hope. It's really amazing.

It's been six weeks since we were here and it's time for the big reveal. I had the tests yesterday, and unlike just about anywhere else, the results have already been reviewed by my doctor and he's ready to discuss them. Now we find out if these spots on my liver are still retreating, or if we're definitely staring at stage four. Linda is optimistic. I am too, but just a bit less.

"Let's be honest, we've already seen these spots shrink the last time we were here. There's no reason to believe that they haven't become even smaller," she says with a defiant certainty.

"I know. I know you're right."

I hope she's right.

Dr. Red Sox doesn't waste any time getting to the results. I like that about him.

"Your tests confirm that the lesions are shrinking. They are not cancerous. If they were, and you were getting that type of result from just Tarceva, then you need to contact the company and be their spokesman, because no one has obtained that kind of outcome."

Apparently, all of the areas of concern are shrinking, which indicates that healthy liver cells are regenerating. The scans also show that there are no new tumors anywhere in my organs or abdominal cavity.

"Look, even though we don't see the tumors, we know that there were cancer cells remaining after your surgery. My recommendation is to use systemic chemotherapy to treat your whole body. There's nothing specific to shoot at with the CyberKnife, and with the amount of radiation you've already received in your abdomen, I don't think it's wise to give you more unless we have to. It'll remain an option, if and when we need it."

Linda and I are thrilled with the news, and we had discussed our strategy if the results came back like this.

"Doctor," I begin, "I'm ready for more chemo. I feel strong right now. In fact, this may be the strongest I'll ever feel. If we go ahead with chemo, then I want you to hit me with as much as I can take. I want to go with the most aggressive plan we can. I'm prepared to get knocked down. This is my shot to beat this."

Dr. Red Sox discusses a variety of therapy plans, informing us of the pros and cons of each. It's empowering to be a part of the decision making process for my own treatment program. After a lengthy discussion we decide on a course of chemo that includes two IV drugs, oxaliplatin and the appropriately named 5-FU (fluorouracil). That's exactly how I feel about this cancer, F You. I'll also continue with the Tarceva. It will be a cycle of three straight days of treatment, then two weeks off. He expects there to be four cycles.

"It's a very powerful combination, and one that has shown some success in patients like you," he states, then continues, "If you're ready, we'll start tomorrow."

"I'm ready to start right now, let's go."

When I began this journey, I informed my network of family and friends with an email entitled "Let the battle begin." Now in March of 2009, after more than 13 months of chemo, radiation and more chemo, an inoperable tumor that became operable, brutal surgery with a similarly brutal recovery, and a stage four terminal diagnosis that turned out not to be, I feel truly blessed to be embarking on another chapter.

Let the battle continue . . .

I'll Have the Chemo, with a Side of Effects

We pass along the good news to our families through long conversations with Duane, Gary, and Dr. Laura. They've been the closest to the situation, and were experiencing the same anxieties as Linda and me as we've all waited for these tests and results. They're relieved and hopeful and wish us luck as we start this next phase.

CTCA almost always administers the chemo infusions through an IV power port, which is a device that's inserted under the skin in the upper chest area. It has a tube that leads directly to the main vein in the area, the superior vena cava. The IV needle is then inserted through the chest wall and into the power port, where the medicine can be injected. It's a safer and more direct way of delivering the highly toxic chemo drugs, but it does require a small "procedure" to insert the port. So yesterday afternoon, I had the port inserted under general anesthesia without any complications. It's about the size of a quarter, and it's clearly visible when you look at it. We're good to go.

You get a choice between two different infusion areas at CTCA. You can select the open area seating with clear views to the outside through the large windows that surround the infusion room, or you can select the private rooms that are about six by nine, and have three-quarters-high walls separating the rooms. We select the private room and it's well equipped—comfy patient reclining chair with integrated tray, TV and telephone, and pillows and blankets for comfort and warmth during the treatment. Linda settles into her rather less comfortable "caregiver" chair, and just then we notice that the chemo drugs are already in the room, hanging on the IV pole. I know this sounds silly, but that's another nice touch here at CTCA. You see, when I received chemo in the past, it was a very long, and draining experience, made even longer by the time spent waiting to begin the process. I had to wait to have an IV inserted, then wait for the pharmacy to deliver that day's chemo drugs, then more waiting for the nurse to get back to my station to complete the setup and start the infusion. Here, my IV port is in and ready and the drugs are waiting for me when I arrive, so when the nurse comes in, it's a quick process and the poison is on its way. I don't feel too bad when the infusion begins, but Linda quickly notices that it's having an effect.

"I can already tell, your skin is getting gray. How do you feel?"

"Not too bad actually," I cheerfully respond.

It's really way too early to tell. These drips are going to take about six hours, so feeling "not too bad" after 30 minutes isn't a good barometer of what's to come. I order some infusion room service via the telephone, and in "20 minutes or less" I'm munching on some of the best chemo grub this side of the Mississippi.

The treatment ends and Linda and I retreat to the comforts of our hotel room, where she relaxes and gets some quality room service while I recover on the bed. And so it goes for two more days. Then we go home and I try to recuperate and build my strength for the next cycle two weeks away.

Before the next cycle begins, I get a taste of some of the side effects I had not experienced in my previous chemo treatments. I don't know if it's the strength of the drugs or the fact that my GI tract is still weakened by the surgery, but I have a bad case of diarrhea. I take some Pepto, then Imodium, and it seems to settle down. But after the next cycle, and for the remainder of the treatments, all hell breaks loose. Literally.

I am cold all the time, needing to wear sweats to bed, under a sheet, blanket, and comforter. That's unusual since I previously wore very little when sleeping. I start to lose some hair on my body, then I get a vertical landing strip of hair on the back of my head that disappears. Linda does her best to comb some of the surrounding hair over it, but it looks pretty strange. Those are pretty mild compared to the two biggies—neuropathy and uncontrollable diarrhea.

Neuropathy is the loss of feeling in the extremities due to nerve damage inflicted by the chemotherapy drugs. Mine manifests in my hands and feet. It starts whenever I touch something cold, so when I walk around on bare floors, my toes and the balls of my feet tingle. When I try to remove something from the refrigerator, my fingertips sting. If I reach into the freezer, the items burn my hands as if I had stuck them into a fire pit of red hot coals. Linda buys me a pair of navy and gray Yankee gloves that I wear in the kitchen when preparing meals and when I go shopping at the grocery store. Needless to say, I get some interesting looks when I'm perusing the meats in the refrigerated cabinets.

But by far, the worst is the unrelenting diarrhea. There's no easy way to say this, but I now have diarrhea 24 hours a day, 7 days a week. I use the toilet upwards of 20 times a day. All I do is eat, rest, and poop. Setting aside all jokes about men and their bathroom thrones, this is insane. I'm eating six times a day, as I'm always hungry because nothing stays in me very long. When it first began and I informed my care manager that I was taking the maximum dosage of four Imodium tablets a day, she laughed and said that that was for regular folks. I could in fact take up to 12 a day. So of course I did, popping them like candy cough drops . . . no relief. She gave me a prescription for Lomotil and I took them religiously . . . no relief. About halfway through the cycles, Dr. Red Sox told me that I will just have to live with it. If I can.

I continue with the program, getting weaker and sicker as each day goes by. I get fevers and chills, I can barely go anywhere for fear that I will not be near a bathroom. The trips out to CTCA on the airplane are highlighted by incredibly understanding flight attendants who "clear the aisles" when I get up from my seat several times during each flight. If my butt didn't hurt so much, this would be rather funny. My weight drops to 170 pounds. I've now lost more than 25% of my pre-surgery body weight. The numbness in my hands and feet is present all the time. I have regular bouts of severe pain emanating from below my rib cage where my liver resides.

One day near the end of treatment, as I'm sitting on the toilet, actually crying from the physical pain and emotional toll, Linda hears me and comes into the bathroom.

"Are you okay?"

"I know that I said for them to hit me as hard as they could, but for the first time, I can understand how someone would elect not to get the treatments any longer."

"What are you saying? Are you giving up?"

"No, I'm not giving up. But if the treatments weren't working, then I could see how you'd just say 'screw it'."

"They are working, you're beating this. Don't you give up!"

When you're a healthy person, and you come down with the flu or some other serious illness that puts you out of commission for a few weeks, you growl at it. You're angry that you feel like crap. You moan about a case of diarrhea that lasts a couple of days. You expect to get well, and you're impatient about getting better.

"I want to get better, and I want it now!" you scream.

But when you're fighting cancer and going through something as difficult to endure as chemo, it's profoundly different. You don't know if you're getting better. You don't know if the treatments are working. The pain you're suffering through may be for naught. You don't just need physical strength, you need mental toughness. And you need faith.

And so, despite all of these debilitating side effects and my little pity party on the potty, I know that this is the price I have to pay to give myself a chance to win.

There's no way I'm giving up now.

And with that, it's off to CTCA for the final round.

Judgment Day

As I sit in the examining room waiting for Dr. Red Sox to come in with my latest scan results, I have some time to reflect on this past summer.

It's been almost three months since I completed the chemotherapy and the recovery has been anything but smooth. The neuropathy persists, and while the round-the-clock diarrhea has dissipated, I'm still visiting the commode almost 10 times a day. The fatigue has also faded into the background and I'm not spending all my time in bed or on the couch.

I did have an emergency a couple of months back, right after I completed the cycles of chemo. The day before we leave for Colorado to attend my nephew's high school graduation, I come down with a slight fever. It's 102 degrees, and according to the cancer patient emergency handbook, that requires a visit to the emergency room. I fight that decision with Linda, then Dr. Laura, arguing that I can take Advil for 24 hours, then I'll be in Colorado where Laura can keep an eye on me.

"Bob, you could be dead in 24 hours. Forget Anthony's graduation, and get to the ER!" she orders.

Linda threatens to call the police if I don't go, so I relent and we head over to the local hospital. I am admitted right away and my fever spikes to 105 degrees that night. Good thing I decided to come to the hospital. Five days later, I'm much improved, and discharged. Another battle won.

I've been back to CTCA twice in the last couple of months, and both times the scans have looked good. No recurrence of cancer anywhere, and continued reduction of lesions on my liver. But despite those good results, I'm feeling very vulnerable and sad this time.

143

My friend and colleague, Lanny, has taken a turn for the worse. After more than a year post-surgery, his cancer has returned with a vengeance. It's in his liver and abdominal cavity. He calls to tell me personally, as he didn't want me to hear it through the grapevine. He sounds terribly defeated and says that his main goal is to live to see his daughter get married in a few months. He says goodbye, and for the first time since we began our regular calls to each other, we don't mention when we will speak again.

And last week, regular TV programming was interrupted with the news that Patrick Swayze had lost his battle with pancreatic cancer. We had just come home from a week at our timeshare at a Catskill Mountains resort that brought *Dirty Dancing* memories to life. To hear that Mr. Swayze had died was another big blow to my dream of seeing a prominent person with PC survive and lead the charge in bringing national attention to this disease. Doesn't anyone survive?

As usual, I'm a basket case as I wait to hear the results, and Linda jokes with me that I look like I'm in dire need of a Xanax. Just as I crack a slight smile, Dr. Red Sox opens the door and sits down on the circular doctor's stool.

"Your scans look good. There has been no change, other than the lesions on your liver continue to decrease in size," he says with a big, toothy smile. He seems genuinely pleased.

"That's just the best news," I respond through tears as I squeeze Linda's hand.

"You are in what we call 'long term remission.' Officially, you're a NED, no evidence of disease," he continues.

"Okay, I'm ready for another round."

"No, no. There's no reason to give you more chemotherapy in the absence of any cancer. We need to let you get strong and save those bullets for if and when we ever need them. There are a lot of options left should we have to go there. The less we use now, the more we'll have to choose from."

"So, what do I do now?" I ask as I stare directly into his eyes.

"You're done for now. We'll still test you every three months, but congratulations, you're doing great. Go live your life, enjoy!"

The New Normal

It's a strange feeling to walk out of CTCA with no scheduled treatment plans. For the past 18 months, our lives have been consumed with nothing but this epic fight. I feel a sense of abandonment at the thought of not coming back to see my doctor, other than for the quarterly tests. Don't I need to be monitored more closely? Don't they want to take my blood counts every week? What about this port in my chest? Who's going to look after that?

"What does he mean, 'Go live your life'? I have pancreatic cancer," I say to Linda.

"Had. You *had* pancreatic cancer. Long term remission, remember?" she responds with a hug.

"That's going to take some time to digest."

That weekend, Linda and I go to a friend's house for an afternoon picnic with all of our friends. There are hugs and toasts all around. They are all in such happy moods. The summer has ended, and this beautiful fall day is ending with a gorgeous orange sunset that's sinking just below the deck rails. As I watch that sunset and all of my friends, I'm struck by the realization that their lives seem so carefree, so lacking of the life-and-death war that I've just been through. They can't begin to comprehend what I feel, what I've just come through. I smile along with them, but I'm not really happy. My mind is cluttered with worry and doubt. I'm clearly not ready to embrace this survivor moniker. How do I find my way again? How do I find meaning and fulfillment again?

I find myself with a lot of time to ponder those questions. I enroll in a cancer support group called *Transitions* that's devoted to newly minted cancer survivors, and it helps to talk about my fears of recurrence. I try to find the answer of how to cope with the real probability that the sword that hangs over me will eventually fall again. My group is comprised of mostly prostate and breast cancer survivors and they gasp with amazement as I relate my journey at our first session. When I finish, they applaud. I'm starting to realize that even to fellow cancer patients, my story is something special.

"Congratulations to each of you," our facilitator begins.

"You are all part of a special group. You are all cancer survivors," she continues.

"Over the course of these sessions, you'll learn how to cope with that distinction. How to soothe your fears and monitor your health. It will be different from before, because you are different. What was normal before is not going to be that way again. But it can be rewarding and glorious."

"Welcome to your new normal."

Lessons from the Front Line

Lessons are an important part of life. When my children come home from school each day, the first thing we talk about is how their day was. What did they do in class? What did they eat for lunch? Did they have fun with their classmates? And most importantly, what did they learn today? I love talking to them about their school days, and they've reached the point where they just start out by saying hi and rattling off the answers before I even have the chance to ask.

I've learned so many lessons in this journey of battling cancer. There were a few that seem so obvious now, while others could only be learned the hard way—through the pain of trial and error.

When you're newly diagnosed with cancer, one of the most challenging tasks is putting together a game or battle plan. Usually it revolves around your general practitioner telling you the best route to follow. Then, when you start to receive the onslaught of information and suggestions, it often becomes too much to process, and renders you powerless to act. When you select your path and begin the fight, how do you keep your wits and focus to properly gauge your progress? And all the while, your head is filled with *How did this happen? Why me? What do I do? Where do I go? What are my chances? Who do I tell? How do I find the right hospital? Where's the best hospital? Who's the best doctor?*

Who, What, Where, Why and How? These questions start the minute you hear the words, "You have cancer," and continue for what will seem like forever.

This is where the lessons from the front line may help.

- When you're first diagnosed, it's important to take some time to mentally comprehend and question it, but then let it go. Energy spent trying to answer the "Why me?" question is energy wasted. And besides, you'll never get that answer.
- Fighting cancer is a war. Plain and simple. You're in for the fight of your life. For your life. Acknowledge it, embrace it, and prepare for it. Chances are, you didn't ask for this, but you must be willing to do whatever it takes to win.
- Cancer is ruthless and takes no prisoners. Be ready to do the same.
- The war will be made up of a series of battles. Some big, some small. All important.
- You'll probably lose some of the battles. Don't lose sight of the war. That's the one you need to win. That's the one you can win.
- Chemotherapy, radiation, and surgery are the weapons that you use in your fight, and all come with some collateral damage (hope you're not tiring of the war terms). No matter what they feel like, they're all small potatoes. They're the cost of being in the fight. The alternative is much worse, and unacceptable.
- Find ways to ramp up your spirits and attitude. Force yourself to enjoy life, even if it's in a small way, or for a short amount of time. Find something that makes you smile. Get together with friends and laugh. Don't give up your favorite hobby.
- Remember that during treatment, your attitude matters. Everyone will tell you that. And it does. But don't forget that it's perfectly fine to feel rage. Find a safe way to let it out.
- Don't get caught up in statistics or outcomes from other patients. The only statistic that counts now is yours. No matter which cancer you have, no matter how dire the situation, there are patients who have survived. You have to believe in your soul that you can too.
- You are you own best advocate. Learn as much as you can, but try to avoid overload. It can be distracting and depressing.
- Make sure that you explore multiple options. Get second (or third) opinions. Evaluate different hospitals and treatment centers. Be sure to visit facilities that are experienced in your particular type of cancer. No doctor worth seeing is going to resent you seeking

other views. You are not betraying the doctor, but if you don't explore your options, you're betraying yourself.

- And while we're at it, don't take everything your doctor says as the gospel. They're human, and they know what their training and experience has afforded them. Not every doctor knows the answer. But some will. Never stop searching for the doctor that can, and is willing, to help.

- It's true that to a certain degree, your life got simpler. Before you were diagnosed with cancer, you probably had many small problems. Now you have but one.

- More than ever, people are surviving all types of cancer. You can survive cancer. Think not of how cancer may defeat you; think of how you will defeat cancer.

- Let yourself dream of life as a survivor.

- Accept and embrace the support and love that will be cascading over you from your family, friends, and colleagues. It will brighten your days and fuel your fight.

- Did I mention that your attitude matters? The trials that you go through are merely the price you will pay to survive. Never lose sight of the prize. The reward is too great to be sidetracked by anything.

- It takes strength to survive. You'll be amazed and proud of how much you have.

The Road Ahead

A month later, as I sit on our deck looking out at the backyard, it strikes me how long this journey has been. Eighteen months have passed since our lives were turned upside down by my illness, and all of those have been spent in some stage of treatment or recovery. Our focus has always been on the next doctor appointment, the next test, the next set of results.

We have always been looking just a day ahead, maybe a week or two. Never planning, always reacting. Never calm, always tense. Never seeing with any clarity, always in a haze. And when it continues for that long, it changes your way of life. I try to reach deep and find the person that I used to be, but it's not there. I'm not the same person anymore.

Linda and I have lived the very essence of our marriage vows:

"For better or for worse. In sickness and in health."

But we've avoided the big one, "Till death do us part."

At 41 and 51 respectively, Linda and I are both cancer survivors. Either we've been horribly cursed, or incredibly blessed. I think you know which one we believe.

Our marriage has been strained to the breaking point, but we're still standing . . . together. We've got a lot of work ahead of us, but Taylor and Colton need us, and bring such joy.

There have been a million silver linings along the way, and I've been blessed to receive the love and support from family, friends, colleagues, and even total strangers.

But more than anything, I've been given a gift. It's the gift of perspective. It's the type of gift that comes from being pushed to the edge, and somehow being pulled back. If you haven't experienced this kind of journey, then you can't possibly understand what it's like. Thus, you can't gain that perspective.

Waking up every morning and seeing the sunrise is pure magic. I've become calmer, and certainly less driven to acquire material symbols of my status in life. Everything I experience now happens through the beautifully sweet prism of survivorship.

Now, looking down over the grass, starting to turn brown as fall turns to winter, I think about what it'll look like in the spring. I'm looking forward to playing catch with Colton on the fresh green lawn, with Linda and Taylor watching and laughing.

Looking forward, that's something I haven't done in what seems like forever. But yeah, I'm looking forward to next spring.

After

It's now been a few years since I've completed my treatments, and I continue to be in long-term remission. I'm not sure if I will ever be considered cured, but being a NED is a terrific consolation prize.

Emotionally, it has become easier to deal with the uncertainty that surrounds my life as a survivor. When I receive the great news that my scans are once again clean, it's like being let out early on the last day of school. The following three months until the next screening are like summer vacation, filled with joy and stress free days. Then as the tests approach, it feels like preparing for final exams. The fear seems to be fading a little more with each successful set of scans, but the pain that comes from hearing someone new being diagnosed, or worse, succumbing to a fight with cancer, is still horribly disturbing for me. When my friend Lanny lost his battle shortly after our last conversation, I felt like the bully had just committed murder and was now holding the knife to my throat, threatening me, challenging me to beat him and survive.

Physically, I've regained my appetite and now weigh a healthy 200 pounds. The pains in my side occur only occasionally, and after several months of therapy using a TENS unit, the neuropathy in my hands and feet disappeared completely.

I wouldn't say that my digestive system is anywhere near normal, but with the help of digestive enzymes, which I take with meals, I'm able to absorb nutrients and maintain my weight. The trips to the bathroom continue at a rate that's higher than what many would consider normal, but we've invested in a very comfortable toilet seat. Let's put it this way, when the kids can't find me, they know where to look first.

I still ingest about 25 pills a day, consisting of Tarceva and some other prescription drugs, as well as high doses of fish oil, calcium, melatonin, L-Carnitine, vitamin D and a glyconutritional supplement called Ambrotose®.

Although I still experience daily fatigue from my medications, all in all, my health and quality of life is seriously good. I mean, I still have aches and pains that scare me to death, but my doctor seems to take joy in informing me that those are primarily because I'm in my fifties and not in good enough shape.

"Exercise, dammit, and you'll feel better," he likes to inform me, "but that's what I'd tell any person, not just someone who's survived cancer."

It's nice to be lumped back in with the normal people, doing things that normal people do.

Maybe it's time to head over to Coney Island, and go for a ride on the Cyclone.

Thanks

To all of the doctors, nurses, and staff of the many medical hospitals and facilities that I've spent so much time in these past few years, thank you for your skill and willingness to advance the battle against the odds. Despite my frustrations and the need to search for new opinions and treatments, the medical staff at each hospital helped me become a survivor.

To Dr. Hero, thank you for listening to me, ignoring the statistics, expanding the boundaries of pancreatic surgery, and ultimately giving me a chance to live.

To Dr. Red Sox, thank you for continuing the fight when things looked darkest, and for firing up my competitive juices with your tales of Boston's superiority.

To my many friends, colleagues, and family, thank you for your love and support, and for your countless acts of kindness.

To my editor, Erica Dhawan, thank you for your encouragement and assistance in helping me to complete this project.

To Amanda, thank you for caring for our little ones, and for keeping their lives fun and protected.

To Louie D, Kenny, Tombo, Mr. Williams, Strom, and Bobby G, thank you for your friendship.

To Helen, thank you for all of your help in our times of need, and for treating me as your own.

To Dr. Laura, thank you for your expertise, compassion, and guidance.

To Duane and Gary, thank you for your endless stream of calls, for always being there, and confirming that family always rises above all.

And to my wife, Linda:

Thank you for your care and love, your unwavering optimism and support, and our beautiful family. You have simply taught me everything in the past 17 years.

Not too bad, considering I thought I already knew it all.

About the Author

Bob continues to live in New Jersey with Linda, Taylor, and Colton. He has left the daily grind of corporate life behind, and is using his entrepreneurial management skills in a variety of new ventures.

In addition to consulting for several consumer product manufacturers, he manages a delightful and rewarding children's entertainment business which is marketed over the internet at www.SantaSpeaking.com.

He has been featured as a New York Presbyterian Pancreas Center "Story of Hope" and is one of the patient stories in their "Amazing Things are Happening Here" advertising campaign.

He and Linda frequently speak with newly diagnosed cancer patients, offering them guidance, hope, and a compassionate shoulder to lean on.

He still takes the Corvette out for long drives on sunny summer days, and loves spending time with his family and friends, cooking, making homemade wines of questionable quality, and watching the Yankees beat the Red Sox.

Stay Strong. Stay a Survivor.